# Desperate for More...of God!

*THE HEART CRY OF EVERY BELIEVER*

BY SHANE IDLEMAN

*Published by El Paseo Publications*

Printed in the United States of America

# DEDICATION: Passing the Baton

This book has a three-fold dedication: first, to the wonderful congregation at *Westside Christian Fellowship* in Lancaster, California. They have not only been an incredible blessing, but have inspired me to write this book. Early in my ministry, I wasn't sure how my passion would be perceived—would it discourage or encourage, motivate or upset, convict or condemn? They have not only shared my passion for the Word, but have motivated me to continue. Thank you.

Second, I also want to dedicate this to our children—Aubrey, Shane, Gracie, and Kylee. My wife and I pray that they will take God's Word into all areas of their lives and allow the truth to reach the next generation...to be *Desperate for More of God*.

Third, my wife, Morgan, has been a tremendous mother and wife. This book is dedicated to her as well. She actually came up with the title one morning while we were throwing ideas around. Her love and strength continues to amaze me. She is a true Proverbs 31 woman. Thank you for encouraging me in this endeavor—you truly are a blessing.

# Table of Contents

# ENDORSEMENTS

"Bold, Outspoken, and Prophetic, this book is sure to awaken, convict, and challenge ..." *Alex Montoya; Associate Professor of Pastoral Ministries, The Master's Seminary in Sun Valley, California*

"With books such as Crazy Love by Francis Chan and Radical by David Platt, here comes a book of equal importance for the evangelical Church of our day. Read it and be challenged." *Greg Gordon; Founder, SermonIndex.net*

"*Desperate for More of God.* The title says it all. Pastor Shane Idleman's heart for personal revival is evident throughout ... engaging, challenging, and convicting, this book is sure to revive the hearts of those who are truly seeking God." *Pastor Jim Garlow; Skyline Church, San Diego, Ca.*

# ACKNOWLEDGMENTS

Again, my deepest gratitude to my wife Morgan, my daughters Aubrey, Gracie, Kylee, and my son Shane, all have been a tremendous blessing. I thank God for a wonderful family. They are the true treasures in life.

I thank my mother Diane Idleman, who has continued to offer guidance and encouragement. Not only is she a great mother, but an exceptional editor and "book doctor." She provided the editorial overview of this book as well as the others. The books would not be what they are today had it not been for her insight. I thank her for the many days, nights, weeks, and months invested—may it return a hundred-fold.

I also want to acknowledge my father, Jim Idleman, who died of a heart attack at age 54. He inspired me more than he could have known. I'll be forever grateful for the experiences we shared, the lessons I learned, and the man that I became as a result of the time we spent together.

# INTRODUCTION: Begin Here

One of the difficult challenges associated with pastoring is witnessing the tragic results of people dying spiritually with living water just steps away: "Whoever drinks the water I give him will never thirst" (John 4:14). Although most can quote, "Blessed are those who hunger and thirst for righteousness for they shall be filled," many have never truly experienced it—very few are truly hungry and thirsty for God. This hunger and thirst is an all-consuming passion that drives every aspect of life.

One summer, I took a bike ride out into the desert. I eventually turned around and began the long journey back to my truck. I then realized that I was out of water. Each mile brought a new level of thirst and desperation. My thoughts were consumed with water; nothing else mattered. The calm scenery enjoyed minutes earlier had lost its attraction.

Hope surged when I spotted my truck in the near distance. Within minutes, I dropped my bike, sprang the truck door open, and devoured the remaining water. Dehydration and exhaustion quickly gave way to a refreshing sense of satisfaction. The desperate thirst that I was feeling was now fully satisfied. This parallels the thirst that God describes in His Word—those who thirst (seek) for Him with all of their heart will be satisfied. This is not about partial obedience, it's about full surrender; it's not about trying to squeeze God in, it's about allowing Him to fully saturate every aspect of our lives. We must be *Desperate for More of God.*

We have extreme sports, extreme makeovers, extreme reality shows, extreme everything...why then, can't we have an extreme passion for God? This book outlines key issues designed to spark faith, challenge mediocrity, and help discern God's will. Each chapter opens with a real life communication. These cries for help are not isolated to a select few, they are characteristic of many of us today. But there is hope and freedom. Lasting hope and joy are by-products of seeking God wholeheartedly and unconditionally as a life long commitment.

The fact that countless people are searching for truth reveals the great need for truth to be re-discovered. We must cultivate truth if we are to be *Desperate for More of God*—truth liberates, rebuilds, restores, heals, and transforms.

On the flip side, one of the greatest joys associated with pastoring is seeing others filled with the Spirit of God— "You will seek me and find me when you seek me with all your heart" (Jeremiah 29:13). This is what I'm seeking to do—to fan the flames of passion toward God. This book is a compilation of past articles, sections from other books I've written, and sermons preached at *Westside Christian Fellowship*—the best-of-the-best. We pray that this collection of targeted topics fuels an intense desire for more of God. Though the road ahead may be uncertain at times, the solid ground beneath will never shift. It's all about Who you know. *Desperate for More of God* should be the heart cry of every believer.

## —*Located at the end of each chapter*—

- Related sermon links are provided for *ebook* users. Simply click the sermon link that you are interested in viewing (you must be on-line for this feature to work). If you're reading the printed version of this book, manually input the link into your browser the next time you're on-line. I also highlighted many thought-provoking statements in red (ebook only) and **bold**. Feel free to share these with others as long as you reference this book.

- Group study questions highlight important points from each chapter. Each question will encourage dialogue and motivate readers to search the Bible for answers. Don't simply glance over Scripture references, even if you've read them before... read them again to see how each relates to you today.

# Where You Look is What You Find

"I'm confused, desperate, and angry. My life lacks
direction and purpose. How can I know that
truth really exists?"

*Former Atheist who was baptized in 2012*

Darkness and dense fog forced the captain to maneuver anxiously through uncertain waters. The eerie silence was shattered as he faced his greatest fear. Through the thick fog, a faint light signaled disaster. He was on a collision course; another light was fast approaching.

In a desperate attempt to avert calamity, the captain signaled: "COLLISION INEVITABLE. TURN TWENTY DEGREES STARBOARD!" To the captain's amazement, the light signaled back: "COLLISION CONFIRMED... CHANGE YOUR COURSE IMMEDIATELY!"

Now near panic, the captain signaled: "I AM THE HIGHEST RANKING OFFICER IN THE UNITED STATES NAVY—ALTER COURSE IMMEDIATELY!" The oncoming light did not move, but signaled: "ALTER YOUR COURSE IMMEDIATELY!"

Infuriated that this small vessel would challenge his authority and endanger both ship and crew, the captain gave a last alert: "FINAL WARNING—ALTER COURSE. I WILL OPEN FIRE. I AM A BATTLESHIP!"

The response was chilling: "CAPTAIN, WITH ALL DUE RESPECT, ALTER YOUR COURSE. I AM A LIGHTHOUSE!"

I've heard this story numerous times, yet I'm always reminded that absolute truth, like a lighthouse, stands solid, immovable, and unyielding as a guiding light. We must begin here... a hunger for God must be directed toward truth. Many are anxiously maneuvering through a dense fog of endless confusion without the anchor of truth.

A weapon of destruction has set its sights on our nation, our homes, and our families. Relativism and postmodernism continue to challenge truth, but to their own destruction. **Attacking absolute truth is like challenging a lighthouse. It cannot be negotiated or bargained with. Truth cannot move.**

I don't want to imply that I have all the answers. We cannot assume that we understand all the mysteries surrounding the nature of God—He is infinite, we are finite—but we can boldly and confidently present the absolute truth found in His Word. For example, God desires that we are saved and worship Him, that we are holy and set apart for His glory, that we are filled continually with the Holy Spirit, that we witness to others and make disciples, and so on (cf. 1 Timothy 2:4; 1 Thessalonians 4:3-7; Ephesians 5:17-18; and Matthew

28:19). All of these areas begin and end with truth. Truth liberates, rebuilds, restores, heals, and transforms.

We live in a culture that often describes Christians as "ignorant" and "narrow-minded" simply because we claim that we can know the truth. The culture, on the other hand, often interprets only by experience and feeling. Truth is relative to the situation rather than absolute. Feelings shouldn't lead, they should follow. Jeremiah 17:9 reminds us, "The heart is deceitful above all things, and desperately wicked; who can know it?" Although feelings can be good and God-ordained, when it comes to making decisions, we shouldn't interpret the Scriptures in the light of our feelings, but rather, interpret our feelings through the light of Scripture.

When people, groups, denominations, or movements depart from absolute truth, and, thus, quench and grieve the Spirit of God, they become mechanical in their approach to Christianity and lose the ability to guide. The Word of God is not in their hearts "like a burning fire" (Jeremiah 20:9), but relative, powerless, and debatable. This is what we see today; many are not truly worshipping God, as Jesus said, "in spirit and truth" (John 4:23). Unfortunately, those Christians who are sounding the alarm are often categorized as irrational, judgmental, bigoted, and intolerant. *But how can we warn if we won't confront, correct if we won't challenge, and contend if we won't question?* We must speak the truth in love.

When my first daughter was 18 months old, my wife and I took her to a local feline zoo. As we walked through the facility, we were entertained by a variety of small leopards, tigers, and other exotic felines. One last stop was on a miniature train ride. As we rounded the first turn, I was amazed and shocked to see a large lion leaning against the chain-link fence with his massive paws slamming against it.

As the train moved slowly through the lion exhibit, I looked down, and to my horror, my daughter was unbuckling her seat belt. She shouted, "Daddy, hug lion; play with lion," as she desperately tried to get out of the train. I replied with an emphatic "no" as I pulled her tightly to me and refastened her seat belt. Needless to say, she wasn't happy. She began crying, hoping that it would change my mind. To her, and others looking on from a distance, I may have appeared narrow-minded, judgmental, and intolerant, but had I let my daughter "play" with the lion, she might have been mauled to death. That's speaking the truth in love: loving enough to tell the truth, even if it hurts—to spare others tremendous pain. This is what this book attempts to do.

## Engage, Not Enrage the Culture

Since evangelicals are often viewed as irrational, conceited, narrow-minded, and unintelligent, we should engage the culture while demonstrating humility, wisdom, patience, and discernment. The truth will set them free (cf. John 8:32). We must articulate our message clearly, patiently, and wisely. We must respond to the culture rather than react. A reaction often calls for an apology, while a response generally thinks things through, and often, no apologies are needed.

Truth, to be truly effective, must be underscored with love. **"Conviction that is not under-girded by love makes the possessor of that conviction obnoxious, and the dogma possessed becomes repulsive" (Ravi Zacharias).** We must make every effort not to come across harsh, overly critical, or arrogant, but to speak the truth from a gentle spirit. Granted, this is hard. Many times, I'd rather forcefully quote Scriptures and end the argument instead of allowing a gentle spirit to guide my words. Meekness is not the absence of strength; it's strength under control. It takes a great deal of strength to engage the culture in a spirit of humility while avoiding being harsh, cruel, and insensitive. A gentle response, underscored with truth, can win far more than a harsh response.

Some may argue, "What about Jesus' aggressive approach when He confronted the religious leaders?" First, He was dealing primarily with hypocrisy, not debating the culture. Second, this approach may be the exception from time to time, but never the rule. Third, He knew the heart of those He was confronting—we don't. Remember, you can be right in your reasoning, yet wrong in your attitude. The question shouldn't be, "How can I win this argument?" but rather, "How can I persuasively and patiently articulate my message without compromising my Christian character...how can I truly demonstrate God's love to others?"

I'm not suggesting that we compromise our principles or God's Word in the pursuit of peace or unity—truth cannot be compromised. God blesses and honors the peacemaker but not the religious negotiator. Standing up for truth will, at times, enrage others; this is not what I'm referring to. I'm referring to those who ignite anger by being obnoxious, vain, conceited, and blatantly disrespectful. Avoid this at all costs.

In Acts 20:31, the apostle Paul spoke the truth in love as reflected in his statement, "Therefore watch, and remember that for three years I did not cease to warn everyone night and day with tears." Was he wrong, out of step with the culture, and arrogant? Or was he speaking the truth in love? "The Lord is not slow in keeping his promise, as some understand slowness. Instead he is patient with you, not wanting anyone to perish, but everyone to come to repentance" (2 Peter 3:9 NIV). Even a brief review of the New Testament confirms this. Jesus perfectly balanced grace and mercy with confrontation and correction. He wanted people to know the truth even if it offended. Oswald Chambers said, "The words of the Lord hurt and offend until there is nothing left to hurt and offend." **The Bible was written so that people would know the truth—the truth about God, creation, sin, and redemption.** In reality, truth invites scrutiny; whereas, error runs from it (cf. 1 John 5:13). *We are not called to make truth tolerable, but to make it clear.*

God desires that we examine our lives and motives first before critiquing others. Jesus said in Matthew 7:5, "Hypocrite! First remove the plank from your own eye, and then you will see clearly to remove the speck from your brother's eye." Jealousy, pride, and envy can be catalysts for criticism and division. Consequently, those who embrace truth must remove these wrong attitudes to avoid becoming modern-day Pharisees. When motives are clear and we challenge in love, we are not attacking, but rather contending for what is right. We are to detest division within the church and work toward reconciliation whenever we can, but we must not confuse "attacking" with "contending."

With that said, I am deeply concerned with what I see, read, and hear from many Christians today. They avoid truth in the hope of not offending. As a result, relativism is embraced. Relativism is a belief system that tends to deny absolute truth by redefining truth based on personal experiences. In this thinking, the only absolute is that there are no absolutes. It's arrogant to claim that you know the truth. In reality, only arrogance can exalt one to a level that challenges God and His truth. It takes a great deal of humility to admit that personal opinions and beliefs are wrong when they oppose absolute truth. Relativism is nourished by pride because it values human reasoning and intellect rather than God's Word and absolute truth.

Think about this: is it really a mark of humility to suggest that after nearly 2,000 years of church history that we have finally discovered the real truth—that there is no truth? If so, then it doesn't matter what Christ said, what the disciples wrote, or what the early church fathers believed. They were all wrong. Many may not say this directly, but their writings and words clearly point in this direction. Humility recognizes that we are fallible human beings who have sinned against God. His Word is a lifeline to our soul, an anchor for our lives; not something to be debated, altered, or misrepresented. We can't change truth—truth changes us.

To be clear, I'm not challenging the need to relate to our culture and point people to Christ. I completely understand the need to be "culturally relevant." My concern is not with those who hold to the foundational doctrines of the Christian faith—my concern is with those who are slowly chipping away at those foundations. The desperate need for truth on our shores has never been greater, but we must engage rather than purposely enrage if we are to see lives transformed.

## Truth—Relevant and True

I'm not questioning cosmetic issues within the church such as the style of worship, ambiance, lighting, mood, attire, and so forth. What I am questioning, and what is alarming, is the massive shift toward relativism. For this reason, I'm strongly contesting those who reject absolute truth. We can't seek God with all our heart and reject His truth. Those departing from the faith that was once and for all entrusted to the saints (cf. Jude 1:3) are not desperate for God...they are departing from Him. Remember, relativism states that truth is relative depending on the individual and his situation, not absolute. When a person turns from truth, in essence, they are turning from God. "Truth is that which is consistent with the mind, will, character, glory, and being of God...Truth is the self-expression of God" (John MacArthur).[1] Truth cannot be truly understood or explained without God as the source of all truth. Truth is not comfortable, conforming, and complacent; it's challenging, unyielding, and distinct.

Many of the complaints leveled against the church in general, have merit, such as hypocrisy, no authenticity, very little humility, lack of compassion, and so on. But the problem isn't truth: the problem is a genuine relationship with Jesus Christ. Most are not *Desperate for More of Him* even though they claim to be.

I believe that we can be both relevant and truthful. When people misunderstand and become dissatisfied and discouraged with Christianity, it's often because they confuse "religion" and "rules" with a relationship. They base their opinion of Christianity on how they see other Christians act. This is dangerous. One of the greatest threats to Christianity is not in our failure to proclaim it, but rather our inability to live it out. For this reason, opinions about Christianity should not be based solely on the actions of others. Jesus recognized hypocrisy and said, "These people draw near to Me with their mouth, and honor Me with their lips, but their heart is far from Me" (Matthew 15:8). A.W. Tozer states it well: "Millions of professed believers talk as if [Christ] were real and act as if He were not. And always our actual position is to be discovered by the way we act, not by the way we talk."

More often than not, opponents of Christianity simply isolate the collective failures of people claiming to be Christians. They forget that we are all sinners. From this premise, they presume that Christianity needs an overhaul, beginning with doctrine and the fundamentals of the faith. After all, if Christianity isn't working, then the platform needs re-adjusting. Not surprisingly then, many postmodern Christians use Martin Luther's example of reformation to validate their cause. But

Luther moved back to absolute truth and God's Word, not away from it.

As a side-note, Martin Luther (1483-1546) was a German professor and priest who helped to initiate the Protestant Reformation. He confronted corruption in the Church with his *Ninety-Five Theses* written in 1517. His refusal to retract all of his writings at the demand of the Pope in 1520 resulted in his condemnation as an outlaw of the Church and the State.

The truth is that we don't spend enough time teaching truth (biblical doctrine) and its relevance. With very few "born-again" Christians believing in moral absolutes, the need to address this topic has never been greater. How will we know the difference between right and wrong if it's not defined according to God's Word? **How can we truly seek Him unless we truly know Him?** King Solomon prayed that God would give him an understanding heart so that he could discern between good and evil (cf. 1 Kings 3:9). The ability to "discern" between right and wrong is absolutely critical. God's absolutes are guardrails through the canyons of life. They don't prevent us from enjoying life—they protect us from falling. Unfortunately, many are trying to remove these guardrails.

Relativism opens the door to speculation and closes the door to truly understanding God. It's a very popular and pervasive deception: "Every man doing whatever is right in his own eyes" (Deuteronomy 12:8). The term "situational ethics" comes from the relative viewpoint. As a matter of fact, the educational system, as a whole, relies largely on "values free" and "situational ethics" textbooks.

The natural question is, "What impact has this had on our youth and on the nation?" An undeniable impact in the wrong direction.

Imagine building a house with no regard to the master plans—allowing contractors to build as they choose. It would be an architectural nightmare. But that's exactly what we do when we attempt to build our lives void of truth ... according to our own plans. God is the Creator with a clearly defined master plan. Truth is, without doubt, critical and relevant.

Granted, if we encourage truth, yet fail to relate to our culture by demonstrating the love of Christ, the church can seem formal and dead. This fact also fuels the postmodern movement. But when truth is sacrificed for the sake of relating to the culture, as we see today, the very foundation is destroyed. Truth, the foundational beliefs clearly outlined in Scripture, must remain unmoved and unchanged. Times change, but truth does not. Where are you looking for truth? Are you looking to the culture to define it, or God?

I learned a simple yet profound lesson as a very young boy. Summer came, and I was on an early morning bike ride to school. As I turned the corner and headed west, a heavy gust of wind slowed my pace. It was clear that I would be late for school, so I turned around and headed home for a ride. To my surprise, when I changed directions, my bike felt as if it were gliding on air. I turned and headed back to school, but once again, I was bombarded with gusts of wind that nearly forced me to a stop.

At that young age, I realized what had happened. The wind was against me as I headed in one direction but with me as I headed in the other. Isn't that true so many times in life? One direction can be challenging, and another almost effortless. In the same way, as we discuss controversial issues, it may seem as though we are pushing against the flow of society... and we are. Here's the principle: even though it was easier for me to go with the wind, I was actually going in the wrong direction.

When it comes to contending for absolute truth in a postmodern culture, there will be resistance. No resistance may mean that we are going in the wrong direction as well; it's often easier to go with the flow of society than against it. Martin Luther wisely said, "Where the battle rages, there the loyalty of the soldier is tested." Resistance tests our faith.

All this talk of relativism reminds me of a story of a university professor who told his class, "What's wrong for me might not be wrong for someone else." One student challenged him on this. Midway through his lecture, the student walked to the professor's desk and pushed his paperwork on the floor. Visibly upset, the professor demanded an answer for the student's outrageous behavior. The student replied, "I had a good reason; what's wrong for you may not be wrong for me." Even from this simple illustration you can see that relativism does not make sense. **There are certain "rights" and "wrongs" called absolutes that are given by God to save man from himself.** God's Word is truth (cf. John 17:17).

Some argue that since we can't see, touch, taste, smell, or hear God, that He must not exist; thus, there's no absolute truth. This is not true. When I worked in the construction field, I attended a confined space training class. This training was mandatory for anyone desiring to work in a confined or enclosed space, such as a vault or a tank. I was fascinated and grateful to learn that there are poisonous gases inside many confined spaces that can kill within seconds. The only way to detect them is with a special device. You can't see, touch, taste, smell, or hear the poisonous gas, but it's there, and so is God. Life-sustaining oxygen is also undetectable through our senses, as is our life-sustaining Creator. "His invisible attributes are clearly seen" (Romans 1:20).

Many reject the Bible as absolute truth because absolute truth, by definition, is exclusive. But they fail to realize that relativism is also exclusive—it excludes those who hold to absolutes. People will accept numerical truth such as 2 + 2 = 4, but they don't like "moral" truth. They want the freedom to do what they want, when they want, how they want, to whom they want, which, according to Scripture, leads to their our own destruction. *God's Word says to confront, confess, and turn from our sins, whereas relativism encourages us to ignore, overlook, and continue.* Relativism says, "If it 'feels' good, do it." The Bible demonstrates that the right thing doesn't always feel good, but in the end, it yields the peaceful fruit of righteousness.

Many are willing to go in God's direction but only if He's going in theirs. Postmodernism really isn't about "truth," it's about doing whatever is right in our own eyes. Sadly, many embrace the occult, horoscopes, contemplative spirituality, spiritual advisors, witchcraft, New Age philosophy, or other things in search of truth. But God clearly warns against this in Isaiah 30:1 when He says, "Woe to the rebellious children, says the Lord, who take counsel, but not of Me, and who devise plans, but not of My Spirit."

Isaiah, an Old Testament prophet, proclaimed God's Word at an important time in history. In this verse, God warned against looking to anything or anyone other than Him for the truth. Although Isaiah lived centuries ago, the same truth applies today. **No other decision will impact our lives more than who, or what, we choose to follow.** For this reason, lay aside feelings and opinions as you embrace absolute truth. It's both relevant and true. Feelings and opinions change—truth does not!

## The Cost of Speaking the Truth

There is a cost to speaking the truth and truly knowing God—the world will hate those who seek Him (cf. John 15:18). This realization came around 2003 when I was asked to speak at the annual conference for the American Baptist... unaware that they were about to divide over ordaining those who embrace the homosexual lifestyle.

Within minutes of beginning my message, people began to leave the large auditorium. Although it was clear that I had struck a nerve, the clearest message came when a woman approached the platform and attempted to disrupt the service. I told her that I would look forward to talking with her after the service.

After the event, a large line of people waited to talk to me. I will never forget the very angry 12-year old girl. My heart sank when she said, "I hate everything you had to say. It was mean and hateful!" Though shocked by her comment, I was moved with compassion for such a young life filled with passion for the wrong things. Others asked if I ever received death threats.

As I boarded the plane, I was perplexed and confused. I prayed, "Lord, what's wrong. I'm simply speaking Your Word and genuinely loving these people." The words of Titus Brandsma (martyred at Dachau under Hitler) began to ring true, "Those who want to win the world for Christ must have the courage to come into conflict with it."

I buckled my seat, anxious to head for the familiar comfort of home... but I knew that my life had made a turn. **This gospel of love had, ironically, become a message of hate to those who oppose it:** "A time is coming when anyone who kills you will think he is offering a service to God" (John 16:2).

Speaking the truth was going to cost me (and it will cost you). I knew that my kids would someday be old enough to ask why the hate mail, mean remarks, indignant looks... while most feedback is very encouraging, those who are upset will often stop at nothing to get their point across.

Do I enjoy this? That goes without answer. Although many applaud boldness, if the truth be told, life would be much easier if I took another vocation and avoided controversy. But I cannot. God radically changed my life by the power of His Spirit through His truth. His Word is like a fire in my bones! I cannot hold it back (cf. Jeremiah 20:9).

One of my great concerns is for the pulpits of America. Many are exchanging truth for tolerance, boldness for balance, and conviction for cowardliness. We don't want to offend; we might lose our audience. But truth is controversial—its convicts and challenges. We are not to seek the applause of men but the applause of God. The pulpit inevitably sets the tone of the religious climate of the nation. A lukewarm, sex-saturated culture simply reflects the lack of conviction in the pulpit as well as the pew. Granted, there are many wonderful pastors and churches—I appreciate their ministry, but, as a whole, the church has drifted off course. They have lost the compass of truth.

The only difference between believers and unbelievers is that believers are simply forgiven—they have embraced God's gracious gift of forgiveness, wholeness, and restoration through Christ's sacrifice on the cross; because of the cross, sin has been conquered and atoned for (cf. Romans 6). "If you confess with your mouth the Lord Jesus and believe in your heart that God has raised Him from the dead, you will be saved" (Romans 10:9).

My goal is to share God's gracious gift... to share His truth. The heart-cry of every believer is to know and experience truth. If being labeled narrow-minded, legalistic, judgmental, arrogant, and intolerant is the cost of speaking the truth in love, so be it. But please don't misunderstand... we are to be gracious, patient, and gentle. **Truth does not replace love, it complements it.** In 2 Timothy 4:1-2, Paul instructs Timothy, "I solemnly charge you in the presence of God and of Christ Jesus, who is to judge the living and the dead, and by His appearing and His kingdom: preach the word; be ready in season and out of season; reprove, rebuke, exhort, with great patience and instruction."

Paul is saying to find the balance—preach the difficult truths as well as the joyful ones; preach the cross and the new life; preach hell and preach heaven; preach damnation and preach salvation; preach sin and preach grace; preach wrath and preach love; preach judgment and preach mercy; preach obedience and preach forgiveness; preach that God "is love," but don't forget that God is just. Ironically, it's the love of God that compels us to share all of His truth, including those things that are hard to hear.

Although disheartening, society's trend away from God's Word (absolute truth) is not surprising. The apostle Paul warned centuries ago: "For the time will come when they will not endure sound doctrine [God's Word], but according to their own desires ... they will turn their ears away from the truth, and be turned aside to fables" (2 Timothy 4:3-4). If this isn't exactly what we see today, I don't know what is. **Searching for spiritual fulfillment isn't wrong, but where we search can be wrong.** There is tremendous power and wisdom in the Bible. Many religions and cults recognize its influence, often adding portions of the Bible to their own writings. The fact that people have greatly altered the truth of God's Word is a startling reality. To whom would you rather trust your soul ... God or man?

There are not many ways to heaven. The Bible and the beliefs of other religions cannot all be right. They can all be wrong, but they cannot all be right. The Bible was not written "in addition to" anything—it stands alone. The apostle John, who walked with Jesus, said to test everything (1 John 4:1), and Jesus said in Matthew 24:24 that false Christs and false prophets will appear and deceive many.

A "false prophet," as mentioned here, can be anyone in a position of spiritual authority or claiming to be. The hallmark of his or her ministry is that they either distort truth or avoid it. Wolves don't often attack wolves, but they do go after sheep. False teachers aren't dressed in red holding a pitchfork. They often look the same as everyone else. They bring destructive teachings and lies into the church, telling people what they want to hear (cf. Jeremiah 23). They provide layers of truth mixed with error, but even a broken clock is right twice a day. Consequently, when the truth of God's Word is spoken, people are often offended because they've been conditioned to hear "feel good" messages. "Many, who for the first time, come under the sound of Holy Ghost preaching are mortally offended ... because they have never been exposed to the white light of the Spirit" (William Still).

How do we "test every spirit" and avoid false teachers? It's very simple: determine if what they are teaching agrees with the Scriptures. For example, if a person says that there are many gods, Isaiah 45:22 tells us otherwise: "For I am God, and there is no other." If they say, as many are saying today, that we can learn a great deal from other religions, Exodus 23:24 says just the opposite: "You shall not bow down to their gods, nor serve them, nor do according to their works ...." In short, don't follow their practices or their examples. If a person claims that a "messenger of light" appeared to one of them as the voice of God, we should point to 2 Corinthians 11:14 where Satan transforms himself into an angel of light. If one says that righteousness is obtained only by following rigid codes of financial and moral requirements, the New Testament says otherwise—"For by grace you have been saved through faith, and that not of yourselves; it is the gift of God" (Ephesians 2:8).

Can you see the unparalleled truth in all of this? Unless a person is anchored in God's Word, knows what the Bible teaches, and believes it, he or she will be led astray by error. "We should no longer be children, tossed to and fro and carried about with every wind of doctrine, by the trickery of men, in the cunning craftiness of deceitful plotting" (Ephesians 4:14). It's vitally important that we study the Bible and surrender our lives to Christ and to the work of the Holy Spirit. It's impossible to gain a clear picture of absolute truth without this. Unless one is firmly grounded in God's Word and led by His Spirit, it is easy to be led astray.

Ravi Zacharias, a leading apologist, said, "The denial of Christ has less to do with facts and more to do with the bent of what a person is prejudiced to conclude."[2] **In other words, people often reject absolute truth and a relationship with Jesus Christ, not because they lack facts, but because they do not want to surrender their will and give up the so-called "good life."** They don't want there to be an authoritative God. It's often an issue of the heart, not the intellect. There are enough facts archaeologically, scientifically, prophetically, and historically to support the authenticity of the Bible. From my experience, I've noticed that a truly surrendered heart does not have a problem with the absolute truth of God's Word.

What does all this mean to you? It means everything. The concepts and ideas of rejecting truth are life-threatening because there's no genuine spiritual life in them. Paul warned Timothy that a time would come when people would not be receptive to God's Word. They would look for teachers who would tell them what they wanted to hear instead of what they needed to hear. As a result, many would turn from the truth and begin to follow false doctrines. Paul also said to rightly divide the word of truth (2 Timothy 2:15). This is why we must continue to speak the absolute truth in love. Again, we don't change God's truth—His truth changes us. We must be *Desperate for Truth.*

## EBook Sermon Links:

1. Characteristics of False Prophets:
   http://vimeo.com/65530605

2. Why I Believe: http://vimeo.com/73129703

## CHAPTER ONE: Group Study Questions

1. Why are those who promote truth often categorized as irrational, judgmental, bigoted, and intolerant?

Can this be prevented or minimized? Should this be prevented or minimized?

2. The Bible was written so that people would know the truth about God, creation, sin, and redemption? How does this fact challenge the premise of relativism?

3. It takes a great deal of humility to admit that personal opinions and beliefs are wrong when they oppose the truth. Comment.

4. Why do so many accept numerical truth such as 2 + 2 = 4, and laws of nature such as gravity, but not spiritual truth? List a few examples.

5. Do you agree that there is a price to pay when speaking the truth in love? What might that price be? Give examples.

# Can't We All Just Get Along?

"Why are Christians and other religions so
divided? Why can't we all just get along? Aren't
we all on God's side?"

*Radio Listener*

A few years ago, there was an assistant pastor in my city
who was accused of doing and saying some very
controversial things. I knew that being "controversial"
wasn't necessarily a bad thing, so I arranged a meeting.
What followed was one of the most confusing and
disheartening discussions that I've had with a Christian
leader.

To begin, he believed that we could learn a lot from
other religions, such as how to pray and meditate. I asked
for clarification, "You mean that the spiritual disciplines of
other religions should motivate us to be more disciplined
since we know the truth, correct?" He replied, "No, that's
not what I mean." I would soon learn that he, along with
many others, believe that we can actually learn spiritual
truths and benefit from the spiritual practices of other
religions. This caught me off guard. I don't believe that we
can learn how to relate to God through other religions.
This is neither arrogance, nor narrow-mindedness, it's
biblical. Exodus 23:24 plainly states, "You shall not bow

down to their gods, nor serve them, nor do according to their works." Don't follow their practices or their examples. It's a subtle deception when we do so. When the apostle Paul addressed the men of Athens, he didn't say, "I want to learn from your religion," but rather, "The One whom you worship without knowing, Him I proclaim to you" (Acts 17:23). With boldness, truth, and love he added, "Truly, these times of ignorance God overlooked, but now commands all men everywhere to repent"—to turn to the living God (Acts 17:30).

God warns time and time again not to look to other religions for guidance or direction. His patience is tested when His people do. This is one reason why we "can't all just get along" as it relates to faith. The Scriptures are so clear on this that it makes me wonder why so many miss it, unless it's intentional. The religious practices of the Assyrians, Babylonians, Egyptians, and so on, drew the children of Israel away from God, not closer to Him. **Granted, we should demonstrate a spirit of love and kindness toward all people, but we are called to "contend for the faith," not to contend for all faiths.**

Secondly, the pastor didn't like the catch phrase, "Love the sinner, but hate the sin." At first-thought, this wasn't a hill to die on; it can become an over-used cliché. But as we began to talk, he clarified, "Only God should hate sin; that's not our job. People don't need us to point out sin or mention it." I immediately thought of Paul's admonishment, "Abhor what is evil. Cling to what is good" (Romans 12:9), and Jesus' words in Revelation 2:15 that he hated the sinful deeds of the Nicolaitans. James 1:15 warns that sin "brings forth death." Psalm 119:163 adds, "I hate and abhor all lying, but I love your law."

Sin is serious, and it should not be taken lightly. Granted, although dealing with sin is critical because of its destructive nature, we also need to encourage, love, support, and seek to understand. When we forget about grace, we can become legalistic. Legalism can be defined as a self-righteous attitude that rates spirituality by how well a person follows rules—Christ plus something equals salvation. This we want to avoid at all costs. **But hating sin is not legalism—it's wisdom, and it's biblical.**

At this point in the conversation, I began to ask myself, "What happened to unity—why don't we agree on these important issues? What am I missing?" John 18:37 was a great comfort at this time. Jesus, standing before Pontius Pilate, made this powerful declaration, "The reason I was born and came into the world is to testify to the truth. Everyone on the side of truth listens to me" (NIV). Jesus implied that there are "sides"; the side of truth and the side of error; the side of good and the side of evil; the side of wrong and the side of right. This statement is an irritant in the eyes of our tolerant culture. It challenges by asking, "What side are you on?" As pointed out in Chapter One, opposing teams can't "all just get along."

## Who Do You Fear—God or Man?

As the conversation progressed, he then made an unforgettable statement, "We should also avoid mentioning the fear of the Lord. It makes people feel uncomfortable." Just writing that sentence makes me feel uncomfortable. The *fear of the Lord* is mentioned frequently throughout the Bible as the beginning of knowledge, wisdom, and understanding. "The LORD takes pleasure in those who fear Him..." (Psalm 147:11).

Fearing the Lord isn't the type of fear one would have toward an abusive father, but rather, it's the type of fear that involves respect and reverence for God. For example, I fear jumping off a 100-story building because I respect gravity. Fear, in this sense, is good and God-given, it protects us. 2 Chronicles 19:9 reminds us that we should "act in the fear of the LORD, faithfully and with a loyal heart." Psalm 25:14 declares, "The secret of the LORD is with those who fear Him." Proverbs 1:7 adds, "The fear of the LORD is the beginning of knowledge."

Fear can also motivate a person to repent. Jesus said, "Do not fear those who kill the body but cannot kill the soul. But rather fear Him who is able to destroy both soul and body in hell" (Matthew 10:28). *Jesus spoke more on the fear of hell than on the glory of heaven.* "That makes me both love Him and fear Him! I love Him because He is my Savior, and I fear Him because He is my Judge" (A.W. Tozer).

The present condition of the church (and America) leads one to wonder if this lack of fearing the Lord is contributing to her spiritually dead condition: "I know your works: you are neither cold nor hot. Would that you were either cold or hot! So, because you are lukewarm, and neither hot nor cold, I will spit you out of my mouth. For you say, I am rich, I have prospered, and I need nothing, not realizing that you are wretched, pitiable, poor, blind, and naked" (Revelation 3:15-17).

A healthy respect of God (fear) is what our culture, and the church, desperately need. Please don't misunderstand: there are great churches doing wonderful things. God is still working through His people. I'm referring to the church collectively, as a whole.

Sadly, there are a growing number of leaders within the church who have left the fear of the Lord. They believe that we should avoid mentioning fear because it makes people feel uncomfortable. **Many of the pulpits fail to stand as beacons pointing people to Christ and the fear of the Lord, but instead, act as politically correct platforms that challenge nothing and offend no one.** In the same way that a beacon ensures safe navigation through dark waters, the church is to cast the light of God's Word out into a dark and dying world warning of the dangers ahead. "The Lord takes pleasure in those who fear Him..." (Psalm 147:11). Joshua encouraged the people to "fear the Lord and serve him with all faithfulness" (24:14).

In his book on systematic theology, Wayne Grudem comments, "We must realize that not all churches will respond well to influences that would bring them to greater purity. Sometimes, in spite of a few faithful Christians within a church, its dominant direction will be set by others who are determined to lead it on another course." Grudem continues, "Unless God graciously intervenes to bring reformation, some of these churches will become cults, and others will just die and close their doors. But more commonly these churches will simply drift into liberal Protestantism."[3]

It's clear from Genesis to Revelation that we are to "serve the Lord with fear and rejoice with trembling" (Psalm 2:11). The overall direction of the church away from the fear of the Lord is a sad reality. It is an indication that we may fear men more than God. Those who avoid teaching the fear of the Lord to soften the message are missing the balance. We are running from the very thing we need: "Fear God and give Him glory, because the hour of His judgment has come" (Revelation 14:7). Acts 9:31 says that the early church walked "in the fear of the Lord and in the comfort of the Holy Spirit." Did you catch that: the church was powerful and multiplied because they walked in the fear of God (not man), and in the power of the Holy Spirit. Paul reminds us in Philippians 2:12 that we should work out (not work for) our own salvation with "fear and trembling."

We must lovingly proclaim the fear of the Lord again in our pulpits if we are to experience genuine change. The fear of the Lord will cause an adulterer to seek forgiveness. It will motivate the prodigal to return. It will cause pastors to spend extended time in prayer for anointed sermons. When the fear of the Lord is preached the world will repent: "Falling down on his face, he will worship God and report that God is truly among you" (1 Corinthians 14:25). A true fear of the Lord saves man from himself. We should take His commands seriously ... not legalistically, but reverently.

It is often either through reverent fear or God's love that we come to Christ and find redemption. The church cannot neglect, water-down, or avoid preaching the fear of the Lord in the hope of not offending or securing an audience. The fear of the Lord offends, and rightly so. The goal of the church is faithfulness to God, not crowd appeal. The church, as a whole, may have forgotten the fear of the Lord, but it doesn't follow that we should.

I left our meeting disheartened and discouraged thinking that we could never serve in ministry together because the differences were too great. I thought, "Lord, what's wrong here? How can we both claim to be Christians and yet understand the Bible and Your attributes so differently?" The answer was obvious: biblical unity is unity with the Spirit—unity of doctrine and unity of truth—not unity for the sake of unity. From this encounter came many hours of prayer and study on the subject of unity. I would spend the next several months asking God to help me understand genuine unity. The following pages include comments and thoughts made during that time.

## What is Christianity ... Why Do I Believe?

Historical Christianity is built primarily on two foundational pillars: Jesus is God and the inerrancy of Scripture. Groups can't be united if we are divided on these foundational issues. This section may help to better understand Christianity's distinctives, and why we can't "just all get along"—although I wish that we could.

We are encouraged to be at peace with all men, even with those who have different beliefs. But the Bible also encourages us to boldly and confidently present a scriptural basis for truth...to be peacemakers but not religious negotiators. We must be *Desperate for Unity* but not at the cost of truth.

- ***Christianity is built on the written Word of God alone.*** The Protestant Reformation set the world ablaze with a hunger to return to the Word of God. The Bible is our infallible rule of faith, being sufficient to give us the sure knowledge of the Gospel: "All Scripture is given by inspiration of God, and is profitable for doctrine, for reproof, for correction, for instruction in righteousness" (2 Timothy 3:16). We cannot add or subtract. We cannot submit to teachings that supersede Scripture. Followers are encouraged to read the Bible on their own and embrace teachings that support scriptural truths. No one, except Christ, has ultimate authority over His church. Jesus is also our mediator (Hebrews 4:15). Although church attendance is encouraged, we do not need to belong to any Church, or Society, to be saved.

- ***Christianity does not encourage followers to "check our brains at the door."*** As stated earlier, the Bible's accuracy—historically, prophetically, scientifically, and archaeologically—is amazing. Unlike other books claiming God's authorship, geographical locations mentioned in the Bible can be confirmed. We know where Jerusalem and many other cities are located. We know, for fact, that the kings and kingdoms mentioned in the Bible existed. We know for a fact that the prophetic accuracy of the Bible is astonishing, as is the internal consistency: written over 1500 years on three different continents by forty different authors saying the same thing. The challenge with believing both the Bible and other books claiming God's authorship is that they cannot all be right—they contradict each other at every turn.

- *Unlike other religions, Christianity teaches that there are no living prophets after the New Testament period whose words supersede, or equal, the Bible.* There is no new truth; if it's new, it's not true. I'm not challenging the gift of prophecy here; I'm challenging false prophets. If a person claims that a messenger appeared to them with new truth, like many religions do, we should point them to Paul's words, "But even if we, or an angel from heaven, should preach to you a gospel contrary to what we have preached to you, he is to be accursed" (Galatians 1:8).

- *Christianity recognizes and promotes the deity of Christ.* "In the beginning was the Word, and the Word was with God, and the Word was God. He was in the beginning with God" (John 1:1-2). The term "Son of God" is used often as a description of Christ's deity. For example, in John 5:17 Jesus says, "My Father is working until now and I Myself am working." Many offshoots of Christianity develop for the sole purpose of eliminating the deity of Christ; suggesting that salvation comes through works and not faith alone. Christians believe everything that Jesus claimed about Himself, whereas many other groups systematically set out to eliminate evidence for the deity of Christ. Making Him a creature rather than the Creator. Christ is not "a god," but "the God."

- *Christianity believes in redemption through Christ alone.* "For by grace you have been saved through faith, and that not of yourselves; it is the gift of God" (Ephesians 2:8). There are no co-redeemers or mediators to assist in redemption. Instead of teaching believers to rest in Christ by faith alone, other groups often promote "good works" and other deviations from Scripture. Followers remain dependent on their church, group, or affiliation, even after death; whereas Christians remain dependant upon God. We recognize that He is the Creator and we are His creation. Any time we minimize Christ, or the attributes of God, we are on very dangerous ground.

- *Historical Christianity believes that Jesus is the only way, the only truth, and the only life.* No one comes to the Father except through Him (cf. John 14:6). We are totally forgiven when we repent and confess Christ as Lord. No punishment remains (cf. Romans 3:24-25). God the Father was never like us and we will never be like Him. This dangerous view exalts man.

We can stand before God because our sin debt is paid in full ... no intercessors, mediators, or works can add to Christ's finished work on the cross. Romans 10:9 states, "If you confess with your mouth the Lord Jesus and believe in your heart that God has raised Him from the dead, you will be saved." Again, groups can't be united if we are divided on these foundational issues.

# Unity from a Biblical Perspective

Without question, the need to understand true biblical unity is a pressing issue. In one sense, the church is so divided that we are, in many cases, ineffective, and yet, on the other hand, we are compromising in so many areas that we are grieving and quenching the Spirit and becoming unproductive. For this reason, it's vitally important that we understand unity from a biblical perspective. One thing it is not—it is not unity for the sake of unity.

The following section is not an exhaustive study on correction, disunity, or confrontation, nor is it a step-by-step guide to resolving conflict. The goal of this section is to briefly understand biblical unity. With that said, consider the following:

1] Biblical unity encourages us to remove the plank from our eye first. In Matthew 7:5, Jesus said, "Hypocrite! First remove the plank from your own eye, and then you will see clearly to remove the speck from your brother's eye." Our sinful tendency is to point out the flaws in others. With this in mind, a first step toward genuine unity begins with removing our plank first. Our selfish pride can create division. Did you catch that? It's not the enemy, though he causes division; it's not false teachers, though they cause division … it is pride (e.g., needing to be "right"). That's why the New Testament encourages us to err on the side of grace, not judgment. **It takes humble, broken people to admit that they need to remove things from their own lives before critiquing and instructing others.** This doesn't mean that we should simply look the other way, but, as John Calvin (1509-1564) said, we should "refrain from an undue eagerness to judge."[4] Before critiquing or confronting, we're instructed to first look within. Is jealousy, envy, bitterness, or unrighteous anger influencing my attitude? Do I have a critical spirit? Many times, those emotions are influencing our critique of others. We may be jealous of those who share our interests—authors get jealous of authors, athletes of athletes, doctors of doctors, pastors of pastors, and so on. **Humility is a vital first step toward seeking God. He guides the humble and teaches them His way (cf. Psalm 25:9).**

2] In some cases, God clearly instructs us to confront. In other cases, He encourages us to turn the other cheek; however, our motives must stem from a right heart. Wrong motives, arrogance, and a critical spirit prevent unity and cloud our ability to see clearly. It's important to ask, "Is the main goal of my constructive criticism to show and display my knowledge and self-righteousness, or is to lovingly encourage the person to re-think his position?" The criminal and the surgeon both use a knife—one to help, the other to harm. But how do you check motives? Here are a few helpful questions if we answer honestly: Will I keep the confrontation to myself and avoid gossiping? Do I take pleasure in confronting? Am I known as a confrontational person? Am I a faultfinder who rarely apologizes? Do I have a problem with authority? Do I have the "I'll show you mentality"? Is the confrontation fueled by a sinful impulse—jealousy, anger, envy, pride, etc.? Do I need to confront, or can I wait on the Lord and pray for clarification? Answers to these types of questions reveal a great deal about personal motives. Confrontation may need to take place but not until motives and attitudes are clearly understood and repentance (if warranted) occurs. Don't move too quickly when confronting (there are exceptions). Instead, patiently wait on the Lord and pray about the situation. *Confrontation must come from a true desire to help, not from self-glorification or self-righteousness.* Difficult as it may seem, it can be done if we check our reasons for confronting and remove the plank through humility, prayer, and brokenness—confession of sin, forgiving others, etc. **I rarely hear, "I moved too slowly" when confronting, but I do hear, "I moved too quickly."**

3] Biblical unity involves a proper view of success. God has called all of us to minister to one another. Some may have the calling of a professional, a technician, a pastor, a contractor, and/or one of the highest callings of all, a parent; yet, they still lack fulfillment and genuine unity, largely because of their definition of success. For example, a singer may promote her music year after year, but her career never takes off. They see other artists succeeding and wonder why they are not; envy prohibits unity. The same example could be used for authors, ministries, and businesses. Maybe the question shouldn't be, "Why am I not succeeding?" but rather, "Am I pursuing my God-given purpose?" In other words, how are we measuring success? Maybe we should redefine our definition of success. Is there a difference between a musician who sells millions of CDs worldwide or an author who sells millions of books compared to those who sing at church, touch dozens of lives, and who attend to the daily needs of his or her family? Society may believe that there is a huge difference—one is a "success," the other is not, but God looks at the heart rather than the outward appearance (cf. 1 Samuel 16:7). It may be that both are successful in His eyes. Surely He blesses some people with prosperity and recognition, but, in many cases, the one who appears least is actually greater. As Oswald Chambers states: "God buries His men [and women] in the midst of paltry things, no monuments are erected to them; they are ignored, not because they are unworthy, but because they are in the place where they cannot be seen." Be careful how you measure success. Are you trying to be the best, or trying to do your best? Doing your best, and being the best spring from different motives. When we try to "be the best," we may have the tendency to compete and compromise unity, thus lowering our standards in the pursuit of being number one. Strive for excellence and make every effort to accomplish your goals, but test your motives (cf. Colossians 3:23).

4] Biblical unity is not "unity for the sake of unity." Here's where many are confused: again, biblical unity is unity with the Spirit—unity of doctrine, unity of truth, and unity of faith in Christ—not unity for the sake of unity. **The next time you struggle with disunity remember that the Holy Spirit is never divided.** Search your heart and try to discover if the source of the conflict is you; however, some conflict and disunity actually promote unity. Let me explain. In Romans 16:17, the apostle Paul says, "Now I urge you, brethren, note those who cause divisions and offenses, contrary to the doctrine which you learned, and avoid them." And John Gill (1697-1771), commenting on Jesus' words in Matthew 18:17, said that if a person has been "rebuked without success," that "his company is to be shunned, and intimate friendship with them is to be avoided."[5]

Wait a minute…are Paul and Jesus actually encouraging disunity? Yes, as it relates to divisiveness, unrepentant sin, and/or spreading false doctrine. But keep in mind that these Scriptures must be under-girded with love. Many churches have fallen prey to legalism and judgmentalism by not balancing these commands with humility and love. Recall Ravi's words, "Conviction that is not under-girded by love makes the possessor of that conviction obnoxious, and the dogma possessed becomes repulsive." **When we separate from those who are unrepentant, who teach false doctrine, or who cause disunity, we are united with God even though we are not united with them.** Nevertheless, there are exceptions. For instance, parents may handle a wayward daughter or prodigal son much differently than they would handle a so-called "friend" who is divisive and troublesome. And a pastor may handle an immature believer much differently than a seasoned "religious" person who is causing division within the church. Not all situations fall under the same umbrella, nor is there a blanket statement that will cover all issues. Again, wisdom is the key. Sound doctrine, humility, and genuine faith are the foundations of unity. We can't be united if we don't agree on truth. Doctrine, though it may sound boring and "religious," describes in words and terms the heart of God. Pastor John Piper, however, offers a word of caution here, "You can become so obsessed with doctrinal error that you lose the ability to rejoice in doctrinal truth."

41

In other words, seek to be united with the Spirit first and foremost—be a peacemaker rather than a religious negotiator.

5] Biblical unity encourages us to avoid relationships that take us in the wrong direction. 2 Thessalonians 3:14-15 states: "And if anyone does not obey our word in this epistle, note that person and do not keep company with him, that he may be ashamed." Paul continues, "Yet do not count him as an enemy, but admonish him as a brother." John Wesley (1703-1791), commenting on this passage, said, "Have no company with him; no intimacy, no familiarity, and no needless correspondence ... tell him lovingly of the reason why you shun him."[6] 1 Corinthians 15:33 says, "Do not be deceived: Evil company corrupts good habits." Please understand, I'm not suggesting that Christians only interact with other Christians. Jesus was a "friend of sinners." We are called to minister to others in all areas of life. We also need to put aside personal offences with other Christians. We cannot totally separate from them, or from the culture. What good is a light that is hidden? **But if a relationship is pulling you in the wrong direction, it's time to re-think the relationship.** Remember, unhealthy relationships corrupt godly character and draw us further from God. Biblical unity encourages us to avoid destructive relationships for this very reason (cf. 2 Timothy 3:1-5).

6] Biblical unity differentiates between essentials and non-essentials. There is a familiar phrase often credited to St. Augustine (354-430 A.D.): "In essentials, unity; in non-essentials, liberty; in all things, love." This statement, however, can be dangerous if you *pick-and-choose*. "All

Scripture (not some) is given by inspiration of God, and is profitable for doctrine, for reproof, for correction, for instruction in righteousness..." (2 Timothy 3:16). There are issues that have been central to the Christian faith since the inception of the church; these are known as "essential doctrines." If a person denies one or more, they are walking on dangerous ground. These include: salvation through Christ alone (not good works); His resurrection; His deity; our sin nature; the inerrancy of Scripture; and so on—these are "essentials." For example, there's an enormous difference between a new believer who does not understand the Trinity, but who is open to learning, and the person who's been a Christian for years yet still denies this foundational truth. A faulty belief system should not be overlooked, but we should work patiently with those who are willing to learn.

You may have heard the term "conservative Christian." Conservatives, and even some conservative emerging leaders, differentiate themselves from liberals and progressives because they hold to the aforementioned essential core doctrines. Liberals and progressives, on the other hand, tend to question many core beliefs. My point is simple. How can we be united in Christ if we are divided on foundational issues? We can't. Foundational issues are just that—foundational. But on other issues there is flexibility. For example, I have many friends who differ with me on issues such as eschatology, the Spirit-filled life, gifts of the Spirit, church government, election, free will, eternal security, women in leadership, and so on. Although these are important issues, they are not "essential to salvation," in most cases. This may be why the Lord has granted denominations within the Christian community. Denominations often begin as a result of disagreeing on the "non-essentials." For example, if a person believes that the gifts of Holy Spirit are valid today, they may have a difficult time attending a church that teaches the opposite. The key is to be united in the essentials, allow liberty in the non-essentials, and let love guide in all things. Sadly, many love to argue and want to get the last word in. If love does not guide, one may be filled with anger, pride, judgmentalism, and impatience, instead of love, joy, peace, contentment, and gentleness. How would you rate in this area? Love makes all the difference.

7] Biblical unity encourages us to respond rather than react. Proverbs 14:17 states, "A quick-tempered man acts foolishly." Think before you act. A reaction often calls for an apology, while a response generally thinks things through. Among other things, unity avoids being rude or critical—it seeks to protect not attack. Patience should be sought when others do not agree. **Those who are bold, persuasive, and opinionated will often have to put on the brakes to avoid reacting. Those who are shy, timid, and withdrawn might have to step on the gas to respond.** I can think of instances when I shared something with someone that initially upset them, but they later thanked me. I can think of other times when I should have said nothing. *There are times to create conflict, times to resolve it, and times to avoid it—use discernment:* "Faithful are the wounds of a friend, but the kisses of an enemy are deceitful" (Proverbs 27:6).

We all make mistakes and a "holier than you" attitude is not the right approach. When possible, don't initiate anything with a rebellious, prideful attitude—you can be right in your reasoning, yet wrong in your attitude. It's wise to ask, "Is it the truth that offends or my attitude?" One we cannot prevent the other we can. Jesus said, "Do you suppose that I came to give peace on earth? I tell you, not at all, but rather division" (Luke 12:51). The truth of God's Word will divide; this can't always be prevented, nor should it be. Anger can be the correct response or a dangerous emotional reaction. The nature of anger is defined by the motive. Anger over issues that anger the Lord, such as crime, abortion, pornography, abuse, oppression, and so on, is justifiable and can cause positive action. William Wilberforce (1759-1833), for example, was grieved and angered over the slave trade in Britain. Wilberforce, a Christian member of parliament, was very influential in the abolition of the slave trade, and eventually, slavery itself in the British Empire. If anger sparks prayer and a Christ like stance, as it did with Wilberforce, it can be productive. Martin Luther said, "When I am angry, I can pray well and preach well." Strive to respond in love rather than react in anger.

8] Biblical unity encourages us to go directly to the source when possible. Where are we getting our information about a person, movement, or ministry? Are we going directly to them, and/or reputable sources, or are we looking to smear websites, gossipers, and "heresy hunters" for the answers? Make no mistake...**we are heavily influenced by what we read and who we listen to.** Check sources carefully. I can't tell you how many times I've changed my view after talking directly to the person in question or after hearing both sides.

Proverbs 18:13 reminds us that making a judgment on a matter before hearing both sides leads to shame and folly. We should approach others with an understanding, humble heart while removing any pre-conceived notions. For this reason, I went directly to the assistant pastor mentioned at the beginning of this chapter. I wanted his opinions, not the opinions of others.

These points remind us why experiences, feelings, and presumptions cannot replace the Scriptures. Herein lies the core problem: those who are not committed to upholding truth will look for approval from the culture rather than from God's Word. *Postmodernism focuses on pleasing man rather than God—telling people what they want to hear not what they need to hear.* This is why absolute truth and biblical unity are critical. They keep us grounded. God's church and His leaders are to be pillars of truth.

9] Biblical unity often "rocks the boat." The gospel—the good news that Jesus came to save sinners—is an insult to the world. Jesus Himself said that His message of redemption would be offensive. He spoke the truth because of His love for the lost, and we should seek to do the same. **The good news can only be appreciated and properly understood with the bad news as the backdrop.** *How can we discuss God's love, mercy, and grace without mentioning his justice, righteousness, and holiness?* How can we discuss heaven but not hell; relationship but not repentance; a Savior but not sin? We can't.

I believe that people respect the truth and are hungry for it. **We are to do what we do because it is right, not because it is popular.** But at the same time, we must avoid being a "divisive man" who is proud, unteachable, and eager to dispute. Paul had harsh words for this type of person (cf. Titus 3:10-11).

Recall what was said earlier—it's all about *motives*. Do you take pleasure in confronting and in "rocking the boat"? Are you known as a confrontational person? Do you have the, "I'll show you mentality"? Is the confrontation fueled by a sinful impulse—jealousy, anger, envy, pride, etc.? If so, you're walking on very thin ice. Spiritual pride is hard to spot because it seems right. The Pharisees thought they were always right, and they often were, but their hearts and motives were wrong. When talking about the religious leaders of His day, Jesus said, "Therefore whatever they tell you to observe, that observe and do, but do not do according to their works; for they say, and do not do" (Matthew 23:3). As public teachers and interpreters of the law, they had an obligation to instruct the people; however, pride affected their motives and hypocrisy crept in.

If we are continually fixed on the faults of others, or how much we know, an entire lifetime can be wasted because of pride. God does mighty things in the lives of those who are teachable and humble. Proverbs 18:12 states it well: "Before destruction the heart of a man is haughty, and before honor is humility." We see this often—a man's heart is proud before his downfall, but humility brings him honor. Be careful, the higher up you think you are, the farther you can fall.

There are times, especially today, when we need to "rock the boat" and contend for truth with boldness.

Regrettably, it's not possible to be liked by everyone. When we speak the truth in love, we will inevitably disengage and upset others. Jesus' words, although spoken with grace, offended people. He rebuked religious leaders, reprimanded entire cities, challenged the rich, and lectured His disciples when needed. After all, how can we expose the unfruitful works of darkness and expect not to offend (cf. Ephesians 5:11)? But at other times, Jesus would build up rather than pull down. For example, the only command He gave the woman caught in the act of adultery was to "go and sin no more" (John 8:11). He didn't condemn her, criticize her, or bring up the past. He gave her clear direction concerning what to do from that point forward. We should seek to do the same.

10] Biblical unity balances both truth and love. Truth without love makes us intolerable and detestable. I'm aware that I'm really driving this point home, but I'd rather err on the side of speaking too much about humility than too little. I've observed that most of those (conservative Christians and liberal leaders alike) who criticize, whether through websites, books, articles, or sermons, often come across as vindictive, arrogant, and angry. We must equally balance truth and love. Here is a simple illustration of how love can make a difference: "I didn't like it when our old pastor said that you're going to hell if you don't repent and trust in Christ. But I like our new pastor," a woman told her son. In response, he asked, "Well, what does the new pastor say?" The woman answered, "He says that you're going to hell if you don't repent and trust in Christ." The son interrupted, "But mom, they said the same thing."

"Yes," she replied, "but the new pastor says it with tears in his eyes."

Hell is horrible, real, and eternal. Love compels us to share this truth. This is why Paul can instruct Titus in one verse to "exhort and rebuke with all authority" (truth), and a few verses later, encourage him to "be peaceable, gentle, showing humility to all men" (love). (Refer to Titus 2:15; 3:2.)

True love is a "choice" and a commitment that we make to do good to others; it is not a "feeling." If love is the greatest commandment, it should be our first priority. When our concept of love is different from God's, unity suffers. Love hopes for and believes the best in others. It is demonstrated through our actions and our words. Strive to develop the type of love that protects and defends others. For instance, stop yourself when you're tempted to gossip or belittle others, and turn the conversation if someone is taking you in that direction. The Bible is clear: *If you have not love, it profits you nothing* (cf. 1 Corinthians 13:3). You can be well read in all sixty-six books of the Bible, preach as well as Whitefield, Moody, and Spurgeon, and have a Ph.D. in theology, but if you don't have love, you have nothing. Make love, forgiveness, and unity top priorities. They will not rise to that level on their own.

In closing this chapter, I'd like to make a final suggestion. Instead of quickly jumping on the "gossip," or "heretic," or "false prophet" bandwagon the next time we don't agree with someone, we should ask, "Are these people truly preaching heresy (a self-willed opinion that opposes the truth), or are they simply espousing non-essentials that we don't agree with?"

Christians are fallible and make mistakes. We should consider the total portrait of one's life, character, and ministry and evaluate on that basis. A few poorly chosen statements over the course of many years shouldn't define a person. One's life and character speak volumes as to the sincerity of his or her ministry. We should extend to others the same grace that we desire and be patient with others. "He who is slow to anger is better than the mighty, and he who rules his spirit than he who takes a city" (Proverbs 16:32). Patient people deliberately take their time and examine the possibilities, weigh the consequences, seek guidance, and do what they believe to be right.

Again, we can be right in our reasoning yet wrong in our attitude. Patience allows us to control our desires and emotions rather than allowing them to control us. After all has been said, there is one closing thought: "If it is possible, as much as depends on you, live peaceably with all men" (Romans 12:18). We must be *Desperate for Unity*. Without it, we cannot be *Desperate for More of God* ... its essential. The world will know that we are believers by our love for one another.

## EBook Sermon Links:

1. A Word to the Critical Heart:
   http://vimeo.com/71710057

2. I'm Offended! Now What [part 1]?:
   https://vimeo.com/48350351

3. The Hardest Sin to Spot:
   http://vimeo.com/77180817

# CHAPTER TWO: Group Study Question

1. A first step toward genuine unity begins with removing our plank first. List practical examples of removing pride and embracing humility.

2. Are there times when we should say nothing? Explain. Conversely, give examples of when we should "call into question" certain behaviors, choices, and lifestyles that lead people away from the truth. How can we do this lovingly?

3. Extending grace does not mean that we approve of sinful behavior, but it does mean that we are sensitive to others. Give examples of when you can extend grace?

4. Our sinful tendency is to point out the flaws in others. List three ways that we can avoid this inclination.

5. If the Holy Spirit is never divided, why is there so much disunity? Remember: Biblical unity is unity of doctrine, unity of truth, unity of fellowship, and unity of faith in Christ, not unity for the sake of "getting along."

# Consider This Before Leaving Your Church

"I can't seem to find a place where I fit. I continue
to jump from church to church. I'm beginning to
wonder if I'm the problem!"

*Online Viewer*

"Thousands are leaving Bible-believing, evangelical
churches every month in America! Where are they going?"
asked the thought provoking article. The answer may
surprise you, "They are going to other Bible-believing
churches right down the street."

I sincerely believe that disunity is a major problem
among Christians today, and pride is often the catalyst. We
get upset if someone takes our parking spot or our seat
while other Christians are being martyred around the
globe. What a sad testimony to our faith.

Please don't misunderstand . . . as stated earlier, there
are issues that have been central to the Christian faith
since the inception of the church; these are known as
"essential doctrines." If a person denies one or more, they
are walking on dangerous ground. I'm not implying that
the essentials be compromised. Within the church itself

we are to judge and discern, but this can be misunderstood, and we easily become "wrongfully" judgmental. Failure to recognize diverse gifts may explain why.

For instance, many Christians have different ministries, but all fall under the umbrella of Christian service. Within each of us, God creates varying desires, talents, and levels of interests. If God has called a man to preach His Word, that will be his passion. If God has called a Christian to pursue politics, that will be his or her passion. (God established the concept of government; therefore, He desires godly leaders who govern according to His standards.) If God has called a Christian to concentrate primarily on feeding the poor, that will be his or her passion. If God has called a Christian to the mission field, that will be his or her passion, and so on.

Problems often arise when we fail to respect different gifts. For example, those who believe that Christians should not mention controversial topics contradict the most basic of principles. From time to time, God clearly calls us to do just that—to confront, rebuke, and challenge. I encourage you to read Jesus' words to the seven churches in the book of Revelation, to the religious leaders of His day, and to the cities that did not repent. Genuine love compels us to share the truth even when it hurts ... even when it's not popular or politically correct. Being compassionate doesn't mean that we need to compromise the truth.

Those who have been called to preach, much like the prophets of old, will confront compromise, condemn social digression, and powerfully denounce sin in the hope of reconciling man to God—they speak the truth in love. This is why the Old Testament prophets were primarily statesmen, reformers, authors, and preachers. They ruffled feathers, and so will we from time to time. However, people called primarily to the position of pastor/teacher often have a shepherd's heart…love, compassion, and kindness are marks of their ministry. **In a sense, one is called to break the heart, the other to mend it; one concentrates on repentance the other restoration.** There is often a clear difference between teachers and preachers. Teachers aim for the mind; preachers aim for the heart, will, and emotions—to stir and to convict. Often…

- The teacher builds—the preacher tears.
- The teacher counsels—the preacher convicts.
- The teacher rejoices—the preacher weeps.
- The teacher plants—the preacher uproots.
- The teacher teaches—the preacher preaches.
- The teacher mends—the preacher breaks.
- The teacher is full of hope—the preacher is full of fire.
- The teacher loves to listen—the preacher needs to speak.
- The teacher sees the good in others—the preacher sees the depravity in man.
- The teacher desires to be among the people—the preacher desires to be alone with God.

Often, there's a mixture of both preacher and teacher in a person. We should not expect everyone to share the same passion for specific ministries, but instead, we should thank God for diversity. If the Scriptures are not clear on certain issues, don't allow preferences and personal convictions to develop into judgmentalism (cf. 1 Corinthians 4:5-6). **Liberty has limits—the key is to ask, "Will it build me up spiritually or pull me down? Will it harm others?"** Each person will have his or her own convictions in gray areas not clearly outlined in Scripture; allow them that freedom. *When arrogance influences faith, we can become judgmental. But at the same time, judging "rightly" means that we filter everything through God's Word.*

Absolute truth transcends our human fallibility and reasoning. Sadly, many today are using language and cultural differences to validate postmodernism and to deny absolute truth. But gravity is still gravity whether in America, China, or the deserts of Africa, and truth is still truth whether someone speaks Swahili, Aramaic, or English.

Again, a spirit of compassion and understanding should move us, not judgmentalism. It's often not *what* we say but *how* we say it that tilts the scale. Admittedly, I've failed in this area because I did not exercise grace at opportune times. We should not excuse sin in exchange for tolerance—extending grace does not mean approving of sinful behavior, but it does mean extending compassion.

You've heard the expression, "Love is blind," but a critical, judgmental attitude also blinds clear thinking. This is why it's vital to seek feedback from those you trust. Invite their thoughts about the situation from their perspectives, which can be a tremendous help. Proverbs 15:22 confirms that plans can go wrong simply because we fail to ask for godly advice. For example, I sent excerpts of this book to dozens of pastors, Christian leaders, and friends for feedback. After the final editing process, I felt confident that the book was well balanced. Granted, this won't prevent criticism, but there's peace of mind because godly counsel was sought.

Wise counselors offer guidance and correct observations. We need them, or we might be inclined to lean on our emotions, insights, thoughts, and cultural trends. But don't find someone to simply confirm your views. **You may ask for advice until you hear what you want to hear and not what you need to hear.** Additionally, don't alter the truth in order to manipulate an answer. When we are honest and open, others can make an accurate assessment.

## Before Leaving Your Church

When the word "purity" is used, most people associate it with sexual purity, but purity affects all areas of life. It's defined as "freedom from adulteration or contamination." God also desires purity of heart—to be free from contaminants such as bitterness, judgmentalism, envy, pride and so on. "Blessed are the pure in heart, for they shall see God" (Matthew 5:8).

In short, how we treat fellow believers plays a role in seeking God with all of our heart. A significant number of people are switching churches and/or discarding relationships. I've found that judging instead of loving often plays a role as seen in a recent correspondence, "I continue to move from church to church. I can't seem to find a place where I fit. I'm beginning to wonder if I'm the problem!" This is an honest question that deserves a closer look. Here are a few points to consider before leaving a church or discarding fellowship:

a) *Do the leaders, and the pastors, view the Scriptures as inerrant—the final authority?* This is stating the obvious, but it's worth stating: if pastors, teachers, or preachers challenge the authority or authenticity of the Word of God, they should step away from leadership. I'm not referring to differences over non-essential issues; I'm referring to those who disregard the clear commands of Scripture. Read Jeremiah 23 to gain a sense of God's thoughts toward leaders who lead the people astray. If the leadership is not solid in this area, there are biblical grounds to fellowship elsewhere.

Some may ask, but what if the pastor is no longer studying and his teaching reflects it? Or, what if the church is leaning toward legalism or compromise? These are clearly points of prayer. Pray specifically that hearts are changed. Spirit-led teaching is vitally important to spiritual growth, and legalism and compromise drain spiritual life from the church. But be careful not to confuse legalism with wisdom and compromise with change. There is a clear difference. Legalism reflects a self-righteous attitude; wisdom reflects a humble attitude that is committed to God's Word. Compromise often reflects turning from the truth; whereas, some change or turning from tradition is often necessary. Never under-estimate the influence of faithful leaders who value and uphold the Word of God ... be thankful for them.

b) *Is God's Spirit truly leading you to leave?* Psalm 32:8 declares, "I will instruct you and teach you in the way you should go; I will guide you with My eye." God guides those who are willing to follow (cf. John 7:17). If God seems distant, Bible study boring, and church irrelevant, or if legalism, judgmentalism, and dead formalism are setting in, it may be that the work of the Holy Spirit is being suppressed. More change will be seen outwardly as the Holy Spirit is given more power to rule inwardly. Sanctification is God's job, but obedience is ours. Brokenness, humility, and full surrender provide fertile ground for the Spirit. But don't confuse a Spirit-filled life with sheer emotionalism or an emotional experience. D. Martyn Lloyd-Jones cautions: *Never interpret Scripture in the light of your experiences, but rather, interpret your experiences in the penetrating light of Scripture.* For instance, we shouldn't make decisions, such as leaving a church, based on emotions alone. Emotions aren't necessarily a reflection of a right decision, but a right decision can affect emotions, such as feeling peace once a wise decision is made. We should thank God for our emotions, but they are the caboose not the engine of the train, so to speak. They follow, but rarely should they lead.

It's been said that if the influence of the Holy Spirit were removed from the early church, 90 percent of the work would have ceased. Unfortunately, it appears that if the Holy Spirit were removed from the church today, 90 percent of the work would continue. Sadly, the only thing holding many churches together today is social activity not the activity of the Spirit. When we fail to embrace the Spirit's power, we become powerless. Personally, I wouldn't want to be part of a church that suppresses the work of the Spirit whether through compromise, judgmentalism, indifference, or disbelief.

The conviction of the Holy Spirit is a true gift from God. Sadly, many people ignore it, yet they say that God is leading them to do this or that. But all too often, they find that they made a very poor decision. What happened? The Holy Spirit didn't lead them—human nature, pride, and emotions probably did. For instance, we all know people, perhaps ourselves, who mistakenly jumped into a dating relationship or marriage, spent money frivolously, moved, or left a church believing that God's Spirit was leading. I'm amazed at the number of people who don't have a servant's heart, who don't read the Word, who don't spend time in prayer, who don't display humility, and yet think the Spirit is leading them. Let me be clear: God directs us to make "wise" decisions that correspond with His Word. *Disobedience leads to disappointment.*

I'm not suggesting that God doesn't lead people to leave their churches, because He does. That's why it's important to first ask, "Is God truly guiding me?" before making an important decision. One of the best ways to know if God is truly guiding you is to stay, pray, and obey—stay in His Word; pray for guidance; obey His principles. Again, the conviction of the Holy Spirit is an indispensable gift from God. We must listen to Him. *(Note:*

for more insight into the work of the Holy Spirit, refer to Chapter Nine.)

c) *How will leaving affect the local body of believers?* Leaving a church can have social ramifications. Friendships often end when someone leaves. When this happens, new believers and others are frequently baffled and confused. As a result, they start asking questions. Depending on whom they ask, the churches reputation may be damaged by gossip. We should consider how leaving will affect others, and, when possible, leave on good terms without gossiping or criticizing the leadership. This can be difficult in challenging situations because we want people to know why we left. Our sinful tendency is to pull others down. We may think that somehow this makes us look better. If we are truly concerned about the body of Christ, we will hold our tongue. Self-righteousness has no place here. But I'm not referring to sweeping corruption and deception in the church under the rug. Wisdom is needed here.

d) *How will leaving affect your family?* Most often, the actions of the husband determine the stability of the family. If a company fails, the president is held responsible. If a team fails, the coach is held responsible. If the spiritual health of the family is deteriorating, the father—well, you get the picture. Granted, there are men who, through no fault of their own, experience failure in their home, but for the large majority, there is a critical need for spiritual leadership. Our country is in desperate need of this. It's generally the wife who encourages Bible study, church attendance, and prayer, while men willingly forsake their

God-ordained role as spiritual leaders. There is no greater investment than investing in your spiritual growth and in the spiritual growth and health of your family.

If the family isn't growing at church, or if it doesn't seem to be the best environment, then fathers (or single parents) need to ask some hard questions: What can I do to nurture their growth? Is this partly my fault? What am I modeling at home? *The primary mission of the church is to care for and equip the saints, but, as men, we are called to equip the home—to educate, nourish, guide, and instruct; much of the responsibility falls on us, not the church.* However, if the church is not contributing to the spiritual health of our family, we may have biblical grounds to leave. But be careful here, there are seasons in life. Don't make an immediate decision without careful prayer and consideration. God may be orchestrating the circumstances to draw you closer to Him. And, as always, seek godly counsel and check your motives. This leads to the next point.

e) ***Do you have a consumer mentality?*** Another comment most have heard is, "I'm just not being fed at church!" On occasion, this is very valid, but it deserves a closer look. For example, if someone isn't growing from food, but others are, it may not be the food or the chef, so to speak. Yes, the pastor has a responsibility to teach the Word, but we also have a responsibility to listen and to apply what is being said. Sadly, many have a "consumer" mentality when it comes to church (I've been guilty of this myself). We come asking, "What can I get?" rather than, "What can I give?" That's why some say, "I didn't get much from the church service today; it seemed dead." I'm not suggesting that this isn't valid from time to time, because it is—we should benefit from the service and the fellowship, but we are called to minister to others, worship God, and pray for one another. Be careful that a move is not prompted by a subtle, self-absorbed motive. *I've noticed that many leave because they are not promoted, or allowed to start a ministry, or because they don't feel appreciated.* If we're guilty, we need to replace our "consumer" mentality with a "servant" mentality.

f) ***Ask, "Am I seeking to be used or recognized?"*** Another reason people leave is because they feel that they are not being "used." Unfortunately, this can be the catalyst for resentment, bitterness, and gossip. They are, in fact, being used—that's usually not the problem. The problem often is that they are not being recognized, esteemed, or promoted. They're not being given center-stage attention. Their name is not on the PowerPoint or printed in the bulletin. *For them, it's not about being used, it's about being recognized.* God desires humility and servitude, not arrogance and pride—meekness and boasting cannot co-exist. Recall the statement from Oswald Chambers, "God buries His men [and women] in the midst of paltry things, no monuments are erected to them; they are ignored, not because they are unworthy, but because they are in the place where they cannot be seen."[7] It's often more desirable to teach, lead, or sing than to pick-up trash, clean the restrooms, or serve, yet our goal should be to serve not to be served. We will not be disappointed if we understand that God desires the heart of a servant. "Those who follow Christ must not expect great or high things in this world" (Matthew

Henry). "Expect" is the key word. God may promote a person for His glory, but we should never "expect" this.

Am I leaving my church simply because I'm not being recognized or getting my way? Maybe the Lord is teaching humility, patience, contentment, and servitude, or maybe He is directing you elsewhere. **Don't *rush* when God may be saying *wait*.** When God develops character, He does so to help us meet the challenges ahead, to prepare us for life, and to mold us into Christ's image. *Trying times are not intended to break us down but to build us up.* The only way to build such qualities as love, joy, peace, humility, and patience is to be confronted with situations that require love, joy, peace, humility, and patience. How do we develop patience if we're not tested? How do we develop forgiveness if we are never wronged? How do we develop humility if we're never humbled? How do we develop character if we are never challenged? James 1:2-4 advises us to "count it all joy when you fall into various trials, knowing that the testing of your faith produces patience. But let patience have its perfect work, that you may be perfect and complete, lacking nothing." Charles Spurgeon confirmed this as well, "The Lord gets His best soldiers out of the highlands of affliction." Seek to be used not recognized, and focus on character development not comfort.

g) ***Do you have a critical attitude?*** This could also translate into a cynical or negative attitude. This is one aspect of Jesus' words, "Judge not, that you be not judged" (Matthew 7:1). If you have a judgmental attitude, you've already turned a deaf ear to God's leading—it will be difficult to discern His will. Ironically, I've noticed that those highly educated in biblical doctrine can often be the most critical, cynical, and negative. We do not practice what we preach. Of all the books I've read, the sermons I've heard, the people I've talked with, and the devastation I've seen firsthand, one common denominator was present: critical, divisive people who do not forgive or release bitterness, anger, and hurt, never experience freedom, happiness, or true restoration. Ephesians 4:31-32 states: "Let all bitterness, wrath, anger, clamor, and evil speaking be put away from you, with all malice. And be kind to one another, tenderhearted, forgiving one another, even as God in Christ forgave you." Simply stated, bitterness, negativity, and anger will lead you in the wrong direction.

As stated in the last chapter, avoid being a "divisive" person who is proud, unteachable, and eager to dispute. As we learn the Scriptures, we can become filled with pride and easily see the flaws in others. Knowledge puffs up. Blinded by pride and convinced that God has called us to critique others, we might think that we're more knowledgeable, holy, and in tune with the Spirit, and that God has obviously given us the "gift" of criticism, when indeed, no such "gift" exists! **Be careful here—it can be a critical attitude, not God, that is leading.**

Oswald Chambers said, "*When God reveals the faults and flaws in others, it's not for the purpose of criticism, but for intercession.*" It takes a great deal of humility to admit that we may have a critical spirit. I've been guilty of this myself. The key is to acknowledge, repent, and revisit the purpose of love. A critical spirit rarely guides us in the right direction. James 3:17 reminds us that God's wisdom "is first pure, then peaceable, gentle, willing to yield, full of mercy and good fruits, without partiality and without hypocrisy."

I'm reminded of a news story that aired years ago about an enormous oil tanker that sprang a leak off the coast of Spain, and millions of gallons gushed into the sea. The disaster was a horrific sight and an environmental disaster. In the same way, when we're "struck," what's inside spills out. Is anger, pride, unforgiveness, or selfishness exposed, or does adversity reveal patience, humility, forgiveness, and self-control? We can choose whether or not to have a critical attitude. On that note, it seems that those who have been greatly humbled by life and who are broken as a result, are often the most forgiving and patient people. The lesson: humble yourself, and God will exalt you—exalt yourself, and He will humble you (cf. 1 Peter 5:6).

h) *Are your expectations of the church and/or the pastor realistic?* Your pastor may not be a motivational speaker, the worship may not descend from the portals of heaven, and you may not be greeted with hugs and smiles from everyone, but these are not reasons to leave. As a matter of fact, we should be thankful that we live in a nation where we can worship God and faithfully preach the Word without fear of death or imprisonment (at least for now). It's not realistic to think that all of the worship services will meet our every need. As in marriage, it's vitally important that we don't enter into things with unrealistic expectations. *Without humility and a teachable spirit, it's difficult, if not impossible, to get clear direction.* Humility does not mean that we become passive observers, but that we live in total surrender to God and align our expectations with His. Allow the Word of God, through the power of the Holy Spirit, to transform you, rather than pastors and others. Again, I do believe there should be passion in a true spirit-filled church. After all, "Preaching is theology coming through a man who is on fire" (Lloyd-Jones). Passion and unction should resonate from the pulpit and the church. Excitement is often the by-product of a radically changed life.

i) *Is preference influencing your decision?* When it comes to preference, the questions are endless, "Why is the worship music so loud? Why is the worship so subdued? Why don't we sing the old hymns? Why do we sing the old hymns? Why are we using a band? Why aren't we using a band? Why do we have a choir? Why don't we have a choir? Why are they sitting? Why are they standing? Why are they raising their hands? Why aren't they raising their hands? Why aren't the pastor's messages topical? Why are they topical? Why are they wearing suits and ties? Why aren't they wearing suits and ties? Why do we have so many guest-speakers? Why don't we have guest-speakers? Why aren't the services charismatic? Why are the services so charismatic? Why don't we take communion every week? Why do we take communion every week?" The list never ends. I remember telling a pastor that I really enjoyed the worship service one morning. He smiled and said, "A few others commented just the opposite." Preference plays an enormous role in our lives, but this isn't always a bad thing.

Personally, I think that what many are referring to as racism or division within the church has nothing to do with racism or division at all, but preference. We all "prefer" certain settings and styles of worship. Ethnic groups, as well as age groups, generally have preferences that are based on experience and upbringing—on what is familiar and comfortable. This may be another reason why God has granted us denominations. *There's nothing wrong with having preferences, but there is something wrong when our preferences become the standard by which we judge others.* Enjoy your God-given preferences, but don't allow them to become the standard by which you evaluate others.

j) **Love and grace should be the driving force behind motives.** In closing, it may appear that I'm siding with the church on these issues ... I'm not. My goal is for the reader to examine motives and make the right decision. Wayne Grudem reminds us, "There were no perfect churches at the time of the New Testament and there will be no perfect churches until Christ returns." He is referencing the *Westminster Confession of Faith* that says, "The purest Churches under heaven are subject both to mixture and error" (25.5). Mr. Grudem continues,

> "This means that Christians have no obligation to seek the *purest church* they can find and stay there, and then leave it if an even purer church comes to their attention. Rather, they should find a *true church* in which they can have effective ministry and in which they will experience Christian growth as well, and then should stay there and minister, continually working for the purity of that church."

This doesn't mean that we overlook the spiritual health of the church; we need wisdom. Grudem concludes,

> "But we must realize that not all churches will respond well to influences that would bring them to greater purity. Sometimes, in spite of a few faithful Christians within a church, its dominant direction will be set by others who are determined to lead it on another course. Unless God graciously intervenes to bring reformation, some of these churches will become cults, and others will just die and close their doors. But more commonly these churches will simply drift into liberal Protestantism."[8]

It's been said that people don't care how much we know until they know how much we care. Again, love and grace should be the driving force behind our motives, not winning arguments or proving a point. An attitude of constant criticism is not a positive character trait—it often reveals an inner drive to exalt oneself. Get rid of it. Before making an important decision, always ask, "Is love truly guiding me?" Furthermore, if you're not in the Word, the Word won't be in you. Again, one of the best ways to know if God is truly guiding you is to stay, pray, and obey—stay in His Word; pray for guidance; obey His principles. "God is more likely to direct me through wise teaching than through inner voices" (J.I. Packer). Packer isn't discounting the work of the Holy Spirit, but he is cautioning against "inner voice" impulses fueled by man's sinful nature and desires.

Don't let discouragement and failure stand in your way. I could write an entire book on my failures, but instead I try to follow the Apostle Paul's advice, and I encourage you to do the same: "Forgetting those things which are behind and reaching forward to those things which are ahead" (Philippians 3:13). Forget your past mistakes, but remember the lessons learned because of them. (For more on God's love and forgiveness, see Chapter Ten).

With a clearer Scriptural base now of truth, unity, and love, we can address another important issue—the price of pleasure.

## EBook Sermon Links:

1. I'm Offended! Now What [part 2]?: https://vimeo.com/48811073

2. The Silent Sin: http://vimeo.com/71818122

## CHAPTER THREE: Group Study Questions

1. Why is disunity a major problem among Christians today? How does pride fuel disunity?

2. Problems often arise when we fail to respect different gifts. Explain and offer two examples.

3. God desires purity of heart—to be free from contaminants such as bitterness, judgmentalism,

envy, pride and so on. How can these sins deeply affect our relationship with God and others?

4. What themes stood out in the section about leaving your church? List two reasons why someone may leave their church? Are these valid reasons?

5. How can we allow love and grace to be the driving force behind our motives? Offer a few examples.

# The Price of Pleasure

"I don't worry about what I watch or listen to as
long as my heart is right. Preachers spend way
too much time trying to label what is good or
bad, black or white, when it comes to
entertainment; it makes for easy preaching."

*Sadly, this comment came from a youth pastor*

Some years ago there came to Los Angeles, a so-called
"human fly." It was announced that on a given day he
would climb up the face of one of the large department
store buildings, and long before the appointed time
thousands of eager spectators were gathered to see him
perform the seemingly impossible feat.

Slowly and carefully he went up clinging to a window
ledge, and then a brick, and then another ... up and up he
went, against apparently insurmountable difficulties. At
last, he was nearing the top. He felt to the right and to the
left, and above his head for something firm enough to
support his weight ... to carry him up further. And soon he
saw what looked like a gray bit of stone or discolored brick
protruding from the smooth wall. He reached for it, but it
was just beyond him. He gambled everything and leaped
for it, and before the horrified eyes of the spectators, fell to
the ground and was broken to pieces.

In his dead hand was found a spider's web. What he evidently mistook for solid stone, or brick, turned out to be nothing but froth.[9] This is a good parable illustrating the price of pleasure from Harry A. Ironside. In our quest for pleasure, we often find deception.

An important question for all Christians to ask is, "Are we 'affecting' the world, or is the world 'infecting' us?" A.W. Tozer reminds us, "Where does Christianity destroy itself in a given generation? It destroys itself by not living in the light, by professing a truth it does not obey." The church should not reflect or imitate the world, but lovingly confront it. We do the most for the world when we are the least like the world. No other decision will impact our lives more than who or what we choose to follow... what we choose to love.

**Carnality not only affects the pew, but the pulpit as well.** A carnal pastor still offers motivating sermons, but he will lose unction, boldness, and spiritual insight. The world, and carnal Christians, will love him, but Spirit-filled believers will leave the service starving for more of God. Pastors, if we would make it our goal to know Christ more personally we would preach Christ more powerfully. Are we calling people out of the deceptive cultural mindset or are we encouraging it by our silence?

Americans spend approximately forty times more a year on pleasure than giving to churches and other organizations... a serious misplacement of priorities. This is often known as "the pleasure principle" that guides behavior toward gratifying immediate needs. This can be good or bad.

In Biblical terms, fulfilling unhealthy pleasures leads to poverty—financially, relationally, and spiritually. He who loves the things of this world will destroy his own soul. "Do not love the world nor the things in the world. If anyone loves the world, the love of the Father is not in him" (1 John 2:15). "Whoever loves his life loses it, and whoever hates his life in this world will keep it for eternal life" (John 12:25).

When pleasures draw us away from God ... when they crowd Him out ... when they take up the majority of our time and money, we are in danger of "loving the world." God is in the background while pleasure and self focus are in the foreground. Granted, relaxation, healthy entertainment, and simple pleasures are God-given. They can aid in rest, recuperation, and enjoyment. Thank God for them. This is not the problem; it is the "love" of pleasure and entertainment (or a perversion of them) that draws us away. The greatest battle we face is the tendency to be drawn away by the "love of the world." We cannot serve two masters. We cannot serve the god of this world and the one true God.

Carnality and lukewarm living wage war against the soul. The carnal person wants to live without God's restraints. J.C. Ryle, in his book on holiness, wrote that "we must stand guard as a soldier on enemy ground." The problem is that many who profess to be Christians, love the world and have a hard time separating. They believe in heaven but they don't truly long for it. They "say" that they fear God but they don't live as if they do. They indulge in temptation rather than fight it. They enjoy sin rather than confront it. They compromise rather than conquer. The lukewarm church avoids the heat of conviction. Holiness, to them, is outdated ... old-fashioned.

Please don't misunderstand ... we all fall short. The purpose of this chapter is not to condemn and chastise, it's to convict and restore ... restore relationships to the Lord. Our lifestyle should reflect our faith. **Galatians 5:16 reminds us that if we "live by the Spirit," we will "not gratify the desires of the sinful nature."**

What we feed grows, and what grows can quickly become the dominating force within our lives. Sin is never static—it either grows or withers depending on whether we feed or starve it. A daily diet of violence, lust, anger, and depression will fuel those very things in our lives. Pay close attention to what you watch and listen to ... what you take pleasure in—the force controlling it ultimately controls you. (See Ephesians 2:12.)

What entertains you? What do you take pleasure in? Are you drawn to things honorable and excellent or dark and depressing? Do you prefer programs about the occult, vampires, witches, zombies, illicit sex, and other perversions of the truth? Do you listen to music that stirs and motivates ungodly lusts and attractions? This isn't rocket-science: "If your sinful nature controls your mind, there is death. But if the Holy Spirit controls your mind, there is life and peace" (Romans 8:6). "The more we follow that which is good, the faster and the further we shall flee from that which is evil" (Matthew Henry). A Christian should not be entertained by darkness. If we are, our heart needs spiritual resuscitation.

We, like the mighty Roman Empire that collapsed centuries ago, are crumbling from within. Historian, Edward Gibbon, recalls the condition of Rome before her fall. The spending of public funds on food and entertainment, and the mad craze for pleasure and sport, topped the list.[10] I believe that anyone who suggests that carnality and lukewarm living are not propelling us in this same direction does so in sheer ignorance or is in denial. "The gratification of the flesh and the fullness of the Spirit do not go hand in hand" (R.A. Torrey). We cannot feed the flesh and be filled with the Spirit. "No one can serve two masters. Either he will hate the one and love the other, or he will be devoted to the one and despise the other" (Matthew 6:24). Again, we cannot serve both God and the god of this world.

Are you willing to do what it takes to protect your relationship with the Lord? It all begins here: "As a man thinks, so is he" (Proverbs 23:7). This is an issue that we all struggle with. The key is to recognize our frailty and weakness and then allow God to change us.

## I'm Just Not Convicted

Famed radio host, Janet Parshall, once aired a program about movie sensations that are depicting ungodly themes such as witchcraft, the occult, extreme violence, perverted sex, and so on. Her guest made the point that the church is losing the power of discernment. I couldn't agree more.

I asked my mother for feedback and perspective from an earlier generation, and as one who has studied the breakdown of the family. She had recently received an email from a friend, though much more liberal in her beliefs, who was also concerned about many of the movies, noting that it feels like we've returned to the gladiator mentality, and that we are being entertained by a "hunger for blood and spiritual darkness ... by throwing our young into the death arena."

My mother noted, "The older generation has seen the slow digression from standards of excellence in movie making to movies that distort and destroy, and are far removed from themes of integrity. Fifty years ago these types of programs were recognized as wrong. Although we might watch them, few of us would dare attempt to justify them."

The unavoidable truth is that many are becoming desensitized. **When the Holy Spirit no longer fills hearts and minds with a passion for purity and holiness, there is a general lack of conviction.** Compromise in this area can be well illustrated through a story that I heard years ago. Eskimos in the barren North often kill wolves by taking a razor sharp knife and dipping it in blood. They allow the blood to freeze to the blade. Then they bury the handle of the knife in the snow with the blade exposed. As the wolf begins to lick the blade, his tongue becomes numb and desensitized due to the cold. As he continues, his tongue begins to bleed, and he licks even faster—unaware that he is consuming his own blood and slowly killing himself.

Within time, the Eskimos return and bring the dead animal home. In the same way, the enemy numbs us through compromise. Within time, we, like the wolves, don't realize that we are dying—dying spiritually. The enemy desensitizes us until we are numb to the things of God.

There is a very troubling trend toward moral compromise in the evangelical church. I've witnessed soft porn images on Christian websites, questionable movie clips during PowerPoint sermons, and youth pastors talk about their favorite sexually charged TV show or movie with the youth, all under the guise of "relating" to the culture. God is in the background while pleasure and self-focus are in the foreground. Granted, we are called to be missional (serving and helping those within our community), but not at the expense of compromising the gospel. God wants us to reach out to our community, but not if we fall when we reach.

To be *Desperate for More of God* requires a serious shift in this area. The need for the church to be challenged on this point has never been greater. Society's influence on the church should call us to an uncompromising stand against her influence on the minds and hearts of believers. Being "missional" means that we influence the culture, but often, the opposite occurs. In times past, the hero was the father, not rock stars. The greatest influence was the mother, not Hollywood. Kids once quoted Scriptures; now they're casting spells. What a sad commentary on the state of the family and the church today.

My congregation is familiar with a phrase I use routinely, "If you don't like what I'm saying, it's probably because you need to hear what I'm saying." Conviction is a wonderful gift from God, run to it not away from it. Conviction is the first step toward truly knowing God. Without it, we would never change. Here is the key: relate, help, and serve the culture (they desperately need this), but don't be conformed to it (cf. Romans 12).

Years ago, a friend was asked by his daughter if she could wear a certain outfit. The attire was trendy and fashionable, but lacked modesty. When her request was denied, she shot back, "But everyone is wearing this!" His answer was right on, "You do not follow the styles; you set them." The Christian life is a close parallel in many respects. James 1:27 says that Christians are to remain "unspotted" from the world—which literally means to be free from the world's corruption. Again, are we affecting the world, or is the world infecting us?

How is one to be in the world yet not of the world? We are "in the world" because we live here; we cannot change that. But "of the world" is something completely different. It means to take on the world's mindset—to think and act like the culture, and often, like the media.

A.W. Tozer adds clarity here, "Any objection to the carrying on of our present gold-calf [lukewarm] Christianity is met with the triumphant reply, 'But we are winning them!' And winning them to what? To true discipleship? To cross-carrying? To self-denial? To separation from the world? To crucifixion of the flesh? To holy living? To nobility of character? To a despising of the world's treasures? To hard self-discipline? To love for God? To total committal to Christ? Of course the answer to all these questions is ... No."

We need to start calling compromise what it is; it's a lack of conviction, holiness, and devotion—"What fellowship has righteousness with lawlessness?" (cf. 2 Corinthians 6:14.) Granted, I often minister to people in many different settings and circumstances, but we must be on our guard and not compromise in areas that can quench and grieve the Spirit of God. **John Owen, the prolific Puritan author wrote, "Be killing sin, or sin will be killing you."**

If you find yourself saying, "I'm just not convicted about those things," it may be time for self-evaluation. If one is offended by a call to holiness and devotion, it may be a good indication that he or she needs to seek repentance, conviction, and holiness again. Pastor James MacDonald once told his audience, "The reason you're not convicted is because your face is not buried in the Word of God truly seeking Him." He is absolutely correct. Holiness and devotion are marks of conviction and a surrendered life. They are not options like choices in a buffet line. They are marks of someone who has truly been converted and who is genuinely filled with the Spirit. Without a devotion to holiness, we will not truly know the Lord; our relationship with Him will suffer.

As W. Graham Scroggie once said, "Light and darkness, right and wrong, good and evil, truth and error are incompatibles ... when they compromise it is the light, the right, the good, and the truth that are damaged." **The church should not reflect or imitate the world but lovingly confront it.** Psalm 101:3 warns us not to put anything wicked before our eyes, and 1 Timothy 4:12 exhorts us to be examples of purity and decency.

In our pursuit to "relate to others" and to "reach people where they are" in our postmodern culture, we run the risk of serving two masters. But this can be avoided if the messenger truly reflects the message. For example, how inappropriate would it be for the President of the United States to send Elmo to express his sympathies for a family who lost a loved one in combat?[11] It would be inexcusable and disrespectful. But that's exactly what we do when we compromise the gospel. As a messenger, there are some things that we just don't do out of respect for the message. An important question for all to ask is, "Am I not convicted because there is too much compromise in my life?" This is an honest question that deserves consideration if you want to be *Desperate for More of God.*

## The Beauty of Holiness

In the words of the famous hymn writer Isaac Watts, "True Christianity, where it reigns in the heart, will make itself appear in the purity of life." Psalm 96:9 says that we should "worship the LORD in the beauty of holiness." Of all the attributes of God described in the Bible, holiness is seen most often. Men fell down in the holy presence of God. Leaders, priests, and kings all trembled at the sheer magnitude of His holiness. The angels cry, "Holy, Holy, Holy is our God" (Isaiah 6:3). Holiness is the key to truly understanding God.

Sadly, many have intellectual knowledge of God but few have heart knowledge: "Blessed are those who hunger and thirst for righteousness, for they shall be filled" (Matthew 5:6). There must be a hunger and a thirst for holiness. A quick mental run through of our media choices, checkbooks, and calendars reveal if we are truly seeking hard after God.

The Eerdman's Dictionary of the Bible defines holiness:

> "The root idea of holiness is that of 'separation' or 'withdrawal'. It is a divine quality, part of the intrinsic nature of God, but absent from a fallen world. The basic theological problem is that this holy God desires to have fellowship with sinful humans living in a fallen world. Since God cannot become less holy in order to fellowship with humans, they must become more holy (sanctified); once gained, holiness may be lessened or contaminated by... feeling, thinking, or acting in ways that God has forbidden (sinfulness)."

Holiness is not simply knowing about God—knowledge and holiness do not necessarily go hand-in-hand. One can have knowledge of sin but not be repentant; one can have knowledge of God but not truly know Him. Holiness does not mean that we never sin. Those who seek holiness realize just how sinful they actually are. The closer we draw to God the clearer the picture of sin becomes. Be clear on this point: holiness does not lead to the forgiveness of sin. God declares the believer righteous (holy) because of Christ's sacrifice on the cross. Christ plus something equals salvation is not biblical. We are declared right before God when we put our trust in Christ, not in our "good" works.

Holiness is not as much about "what" I don't do as it is about "why" I don't do something. It's safe to assume that those who live strictly by rules rather than a true relationship with Christ are not holy... they are religious. They may avoid people, places, and things but still be critical, judgmental, jealous, arrogant, and angry—"having a form of godliness." In short, their motto is, "It's we four and no more. We are right to the core. If you don't agree with us, there's the door." This is not only incorrect biblically, it's destructive. Holiness involves truly seeking God versus "playing church," adhering to legalism, and showing off.

Now with that said, holiness may appear as if one is following rules... avoiding people, places, and things that hinder growth, but this avoidance is fueled by a relationship with God rather than rules. Sin is serious; it separates us from God; it stands in direct opposition to Him; it corrupts our character and our testimony; it prevents holiness and quenches and grieves the Spirit within.

Make no mistake, holiness will cost something. J.C. Ryle said this about making holiness a priority, "He must count it no strange thing to be mocked, ridiculed, slandered, persecuted, and even hated." Ryle adds, "He must not be surprised to find his opinions and practices in religion despised and held up to scorn. He must submit to be thought by many a fool, an enthusiast, and a fanatic... to have his words perverted and his actions misrepresented."[12] Again, we are to do what is right because it is right, not because it is popular ... pleasing God rather than man.

Seeking to identify the middle ground between our responsibility (obedience) and God's role in sanctification (holiness) can be challenging, but it doesn't need to be. The Bible is filled with passages about obedience that leads to holiness. For example, 1 Peter 1:14 says, "As obedient children, not conforming yourselves to the former lusts, as in your ignorance." 1 John 3:3 adds that "all who have this hope in Him purify themselves, just as He is pure." And Romans 6:19 tells us to present our "bodies as slaves to righteousness." Peter asks, "What sort of people ought you to be in holiness and godliness?" (2 Peter 3:11).

It's clear from Scripture that obedience produces sanctification (holiness). Holiness is a by-product of our submission to the work of the Spirit. Sadly, many don't seek the surrendered life. They want the narrow road to be broad and the cross to be light. But holiness has a cost.

**J.C. Ryle noted that "holiness will cost a man his sins. He must be willing to give up every habit and practice which is wrong in God's sight** ... There must be no separate truce with any special sin which he loves." Ryle continues, "Our sins are often as dear to us as our children: we love them, hug them, cleave to them, and delight in them. To part with them is as hard as cutting off a right hand, or plucking out a right eye. But it must be done. The parting must come."[13] Holiness comes with a price—death to self and crucifixion to the world. To be filled mightily with the Spirit, we must first be emptied of self. Pride and arrogance hinder holiness. We are to overcome sin, not surrender to it. Holiness challenges lukewarm living.

A vast majority of Christian are turning a deaf ear to the call to holiness. Conviction is replaced with complacency. Their thought is, "I'm just not convicted about that like you are." Often, the reason is because they are not truly seeking God unconditionally. Lukewarm living disdains the heat of conviction. It "loves the world" more than the things of God. A call to holiness constantly challenges our lifestyle—it forces us to confront idols and remove destructive habits.

Holiness will cost the opinions of men. Be clear on this issue: we will be ridiculed, mocked, slandered, persecuted, and even hated when we take a stand for holiness, even by "Christians." Nevertheless, we desperately need holiness. We must turn to God's truth and away from the broad road that leads to destruction. We must repent, ask for forgiveness, and seek restoration. We should not apologize for following God's Word. We are in the midst of a spiritual battle. We will be criticized for following Christ, mocked for believing in truth, and challenged for promoting holiness.We are called to deny ourselves, pick up our cross, and follow Him. The day of passive, lukewarm Christians must come to an end if we truly desire to see families restored and lives rebuilt.

We also must lovingly preach holiness in our pulpits again: "Without holiness no one will see the Lord" (Hebrews 12:14). The prophets of old bear this out as well. These men were sent by God to call the people back to

Him ... back to holiness: "And the Lord God of their fathers sent warnings to them by His messengers [to convict the people], rising up early and sending them, because He had compassion on His people and on His dwelling place. But they mocked the messengers of God, despised His words, and scoffed at His prophets, until the wrath of the Lord arose against His people, till there was no remedy" (2 Chronicles 36:15-16).

Little has changed. Most still mock difficult messages from the pulpit and the pen. They despise the heat of conviction and scoff at those who seek God unconditionally. Leonard Ravenhill, in *Picture of a Prophet*, wrote the following:

> "The prophet's work is to call into line those who are out of line! He is unpopular because he opposes the popular in morality and spirituality. In a day of faceless politicians and voiceless preachers, there is not a more urgent national need than that we cry to God for a prophet! The function of the prophet, as Austin-Sparks once said, 'has almost always been that of recovery.' The prophet is God's detective seeking for a lost treasure. The degree of his effectiveness is determined by his measure of unpopularity. Compromise is not known to him."

Let me leave you with this thought: are you willing to do what it takes to protect your relationship with the Lord? Ultimately, this means protecting your family. The beauty of holiness is that it draws us closer to God. Are you willing to do what it takes to truly know God? This is a price that many of are not willing to pay.

## War Against the Soul

A famous quote resounds with clarity for us today: "All the water in the world, no matter how hard it tries, can never sink a ship unless it gets inside. All the evil influence of the world, no matter how hard it tries, can never sink a Christian's soul unless it gets inside."

**The greatest battle we will ever fight is within.** Our mind is where the battle is either won or lost: "As a man thinks in his heart so is he" (Proverbs 3:27). Galatians 5:17 says that the Spirit gives us desires that are opposite from what our sinful nature desires, and that these two forces are constantly fighting against each other. As a result, our choices are rarely free from this conflict. Don't be alarmed. The fact that there is a fight confirms the value of our commitment to Christ and His standard of holiness.

For example, our sinful nature says, "Party—eat, drink, and be merry for tomorrow we die," but Jesus said, "Take heed to yourselves, lest your hearts be weighed down with carousing, drunkenness, and cares of this life, and that Day [His return] come on you unexpectedly" (Luke 21:34). Sin says, "Feed me more of the world." But God says, "Come out from among them and be separate" (2 Corinthians 6:17).

Most walk away from Christ not because He fails them, or because the Word of God proves to be untrue, but because of the love of this world (gratifying the flesh). We cannot overlook the seriousness of this issue. Jesus said that the worries and desires of this world, along with the deceitfulness of wealth, come in and choke the Word of God, making it unfruitful (cf. Mark 4:19).

We are soldiers and the battleground is the world. Those who do not stand guard will soon see their soul drift toward Sodom and away from the Spirit; toward goods rather than godliness; toward wealth rather than wisdom. The passion we once had for the purity of God's Word can easily be exchanged for the pollutants of the world. For this reason, I take every opportunity to write about making wise entertainment choices. What we put into our mind affects our relationship with God at a very deep level. 1 John 2:15-17 says, "Love not the world [the worlds mindset], neither the things that are in the world. If any man love the world, the love of the Father is not in him. For all that is in the world, the lust of the flesh, and the lust of the eyes, and the pride of life, is not of the Father, but is of the world."

Saints of the past were known to say, "Others may, you cannot." **They realized that in pursuing holiness, God sets the standard, not man.** I'm not suggesting that we sell everything and live on the outskirts of the desert, but that we remain "unspotted" from the world's corruption (cf. James 1:27). We cannot live like the world in regard to moral and spiritual issues. Again, we should continually ask, "Are we 'affecting' the world, or is the world 'infecting' us?"

What we watch and listen to affects the heart—it's impossible to separate the two. If we would make it our goal to know Christ more personally, we would preach Christ more powerfully. For example, if a pastor (or Christian leader) fills his mind with the world all week and expects the Spirit of God to speak boldly through him from the pulpit, he will be gravely mistaken. E.M. Bounds said, "The sermon cannot rise in its life-giving forces above the man. Dead men give out dead sermons, and dead sermons kill. Everything depends on the spiritual character of the preacher."[14] Who he is all week is who he will be when he steps to the pulpit—the passion and conviction of his message is only as strong as the passion and conviction within him. The same is true with you and me: "For out of the abundance of the heart the mouth speaks" (Matthew 12:34). What goes in ultimately comes out.

A paraphrase of a story that I've heard helps to illustrate the war against the soul:

> A young man in need of help for his troubled life, walked to a neighboring church. He told the pastor that his life was meaningless and in constant turmoil. He wanted to make better choices but couldn't.
>
> He described the conflict, "It's as if I have two dogs constantly battling within me. One dog is evil, while the other is good. The battles are long and difficult; they drain me emotionally and mentally."
>
> The pastor asked, "Which dog wins the battles?" Hesitantly, the young man admitted, "The evil dog." Without a moment's thought, the pastor looked at him and said, *"Son, that's the one you feed the most ... you need to starve that dog to death!"*

The pastor realized, as should we, that the source of our strength comes from the food that we choose. *What we feed grows, and what grows becomes the stronger influence within our lives.* **Again, sin has a life cycle—it either grows or withers depending on whether we feed or starve it.** Which dog wins the battle in your mind?

Entertainment plays a huge role in this. *What you think can provide the framework for who you become—thoughts become words, words habits, and habits a lifestyle.*

To be completely honest, the list of acceptable entertainment is small, very small. For some, the best policy may be out of sight, out of mind. You'd be amazed at what a week or two absent of media will do for your spiritual life. Just a few decades ago, most of today's media choices would have shocked the public. Programs that never would have aired then receive the highest ratings now. You may say, "Times change." And you are correct, but God's standards do not. The sin that once amazed us now amuses us. When sin begins to amuse us, we are dangerously close to the edge: "Woe to those who call evil good, and good evil" (Isaiah 5:20). No wonder families are disintegrating—it's evident to me that we've embraced an attitude of compromise in our nation, and more sadly, in our homes. *Culture reflects our religion.* In other words, the culture around us reflects who and what we value. How we dress, what we view, who are friends are, what we listen to, and how we spend our time, all speak volumes as to what we cherish. Are we cherishing the things of God or the things of the world?

The Scriptures are crystal clear on the issue of entertainment—there's really no debate. Philippians 4:8-9 says, "Finally, brethren, whatever things are true, whatever things are noble, whatever things are just, whatever things are pure, whatever things are lovely, whatever things are of good report, if there is any virtue and if there is anything praiseworthy—meditate on these things." Ephesians 5:1-20 also addresses this issue, and enough is said in 2 Timothy alone to silence any debate: *Everyone who names the name of Christ should depart from anything that goes against His standard of holiness.* We must be pure vessels that God can use (cf. 2 Timothy 2:19-21). A pure vessel cannot come from a polluted mind. Years of feeding the flesh will leave us spiritually weak—what goes into our mind ultimately comes out in our actions.

## The Cost of Carnality

Carnal Christians give God "His due" (a few hours on Sunday), but they forget His call to "come out from among them (the world) and be separate." Every day of the week is the world influencing you? What does your mental media diet consist of? Who do you hang out with? What, and who, do you listen to? Is your heart set toward the things of God or the world's influence? A quick peruse of your "likes" and posts on Facebook reveals what you truly value.

Compromise also deceives. James 1:22 reminds us that if we listen to God's Word without doing it that we are fooling ourselves ... we are deceived. The power of God's Word lies in the application. In addition to non-Christians, it is Christians who are moving sexually explicit and violent movies to the Top 10 by not applying purity to their lives. It is Christians who are addicted to porn and supplying the revenue to fuel the industry.

I often remind our congregation that we can either make our homes a holy sanctuary that honors Christ or a breeding ground for Satan—home should be a place of encouragement and comfort. That's a hard statement but it's true. We cannot love both Christ and this world. Carnality destroys our relationship with Christ and genuine fellowship with other believers. It destroys our prayer life as well. A carnal Christian does not pray, really pray and seek the heart of God. A deep prayer life exposes facades and crushes hypocrisy. Carnality also destroys spiritual power and hinders the infilling of the Spirit. It also affects our home life. In short, everything that God calls us to be is compromised.

When Jesus said that we are "the salt and light of the earth," He was saying that we should have a preserving and cleansing effect on the culture...we should bring a purifying aspect to all areas of life. Light dispels darkness; it does not cater to it. Here are a few biblical points to consider:

1. There is no such thing as "good magic" or "good witches" or "nice vampires." These things, by their very nature, are evil. Scripture makes it clear that fascination with the powers of darkness and the occult have no place in the heart or the mind of a Christian. Even more discouraging than the time and money spent on the occult and vampire craze, is the young age at which children are exposed to these spiritual perversions. **There is no such thing as good evil—evil is that which God defines as evil, it opposes the character and nature of God— there is nothing good about that**. God is not mocked. We only deceive ourselves if we believe that we will not reap what we have sown.

2. Jesus never encouraged enthusiasm over things that God forbade. Our minds are to be fixed on what is noble, pure, excellent, and good (Philippians 4:8). There are no scriptural grounds in defense of these types of movies. It is more reasonable for Christians who enjoy these movies to simply admit that they enjoy them rather than try to defend them.

3. Enchantments, fortune telling, witchcraft, familiar spirits, and wizards are always condemned as evil practices throughout the Bible. For example, 2 Chronicles 33:6 says that those who use enchantments and witchcraft, and who deal with familiar spirits and wizards, provoke the Lord to anger. If these things entertain us, something is clearly wrong. Darkness should not entertain Christians. Once something entertains us, we give place to it and accept it; it begins to influence us. Don't assume that I'm not referring to violent and perverse video games as well ... they offer the same destructive pattern. Ironically, as I was editing this chapter, this headline appeared in the news: *Navy Yard Shooter "Obsessed with Violent Video Games."* Years of feeding the flesh will leave us spiritually weak. Let's be careful not to make excuses and compromise God's Word in the name of liberty. **Liberty has limits and those limits are defined by Scripture.**

4. Being selective with what we watch and listen to has nothing to do with legalism; it has everything to do with wisdom. We are to recognize what glorifies Christ and what clearly does not then choose accordingly.

**Grace does not relieve us of responsibility.** We actually live under a higher standard when grace guides our decisions, not rules. It's not about following rules. Let your freedom in Christ, and a relationship with Him, guide you. We've all watched questionable material and have made wrong choices; don't live with ongoing regret. But don't justify wrong behavior by thinking that God doesn't care about what you watch or listen to, He does. We serve and love God with our mind. (See Romans 7:25.)

5. When it comes to drawing a line between healthy entertainment and a destructive influence, follow Christ rather than the crowd. Would Jesus enjoy watching these movies? I think that we all know better. To suggest that what we view and listen to is not important to God, is to alter His Word. We should be selective when it comes to entertainment— once others see an authentic, committed relationship with Christ (although they may not admit it), they may begin to desire one as well. Again, are you willing to do what it takes to protect your mind, your family, and your relationship with the Lord? It's your choice.

Drawing a line can be out of step with the mainstream, but, like Joshua, we can say, "Choose this day whom you will serve, as for me and my house we will serve the Lord" (Joshua 24:15). We cannot be *Desperate for More of God* while continually filling our mind with things that directly oppose Him. There should be a distinction and a difference in the lifestyle of Christians. This is a by-product of true Christianity. Not surprisingly, the enemy often destroys the best with the good. We can get so caught up in sports, entertainment, activities, and, even ministry, that we have little time and energy left for God. We want to enjoy the world's passing pleasures and embrace her alluring enticements, but at what cost?

Today, we rate success by busyness ... successful people are busy people, so we say. But if we're too busy to cultivate a deep prayer life and a lifestyle that places God first—we are too busy. And if we're too busy to cultivate holy devotion that pleases God—we are too busy. *We should never allow our relationship with Him to suffer because we're too busy.*

Granted, we should be thankful for simple, God-given pleasures and use them to bring balance and rest to busy lives, but they should not constantly consume our time, energy, and passions. The Bible refers to this as idolatry. In deep sadness, the apostle Paul wrote that "many live as enemies of the cross of Christ. Their destiny is destruction, their god is their stomach, and their glory is in their shame. Their mind is on earthly things" (Philippians 3:18-19). Many are so busy seeking the things of this world that they don't truly seek God. They may go to church and may even read their Bible, but the cares of this life take center-stage. Our lifestyle reflects the true condition of the heart.

## The Messenger Should Reflect the Message

Holiness and extreme devotion to the Lord are often challenged by well meaning Christians using the battle-cry,

"But we must relate to the culture." But they fail to realize that the message and the messenger must be congruent. The ends do not always justify the means. The power of the gospel … the power of the Spirit-filled life is found in obedience and devotion, not in crowd appeal and relevance.

An example that immediately comes to mind was when a Christian organization used a 30-foot high blow-up sexual organ to promote a pornography conference. Granted, the need to address the dangers of pornography has never been greater, and I applaud them for taking action, but does a 30-foot tall sexual organ really send the right message? Would the apostle Paul and Jesus actually commend this promotional idea? Using inflatable sexual symbols to promote a Christian pornography conference is like using Elmo to speak on behalf of the President. It might "relate to the culture," but it does not adequately represent the message.

With that said, consider a few practical steps to avoid compromise:

- Before asking if an event, website, promotional idea, or advertisement is culturally relevant, we should ask, "Does it glorify Christ? Is it consistent with our Christian character? Will it send the right message? Will it cause others to stumble or think less of the gospel?"

- Make sure, without a shadow of doubt, that God is leading you. For example, it may not be wise for most men to minister inside of a porn convention. Guys are very visual and the distractions would be endless. **Again, God wants us to reach out to our community, but not if we fall when we reach.** Use wisdom, think things through, and ask, "Is God truly directing me? Are my actions consistent with Scripture? Is this wise?"

- Seek godly counsel on a regular basis from mature believers who can help direct your steps, examine motives, and offer sincere advice. All that we do and say should reflect the integrity and seriousness of our message (cf. Titus 2:7).

- Look to the Word first and foremost for direction, wisdom, and discernment. Many of the questions about being culturally relevant could be answered if we simply looked to God's Word instead of the world for the answers. God's Word is truth for all men for all time.

In general, our culture is looking for authenticity— even it understands that a compromised life sends a compromised message. Again, A.W. Tozer noted, "Where does Christianity destroy itself in a given generation? It destroys itself by not living in the light, by professing a truth it does not obey." What an insightful perspective, especially for us today. I believe this is one reason why the church has experienced a mass exodus of young people. They are tired of hypocrisy and compromise... they want real answers, authentic Christianity, and life-changing experiences.

We cannot make excuses and compromise God's Word under the pretext of relating to our culture ... our culture doesn't need more of the same. "What is being advocated is not so much a new kind of Christian in a new emerging church, but a church that is so submerging itself in the culture that it risks hopeless compromise?" (D.A. Carson).[15] In John 15:19, Jesus said, "If you were of the world, the world would love its own. Yet because you are not of the world, but I chose you out of the world, therefore the world hates you." In short, if we are of this world the world will love us, but if we are truly His followers, the world will hate us when we embrace His truth.

This begs the question, "Does the world love the way you do church? Do they appreciate that your church never challenges, or calls things into question? Do they like the fact that your church never makes them feel uncomfortable or offended? Are they grateful that you never discuss controversial issues?" If so, you may want to reconsider Jesus' words that true disciples will be hated by the world. Obviously, I'm not saying that churches shouldn't be welcoming, loving, accepting, friendly, warm, hospitable places of worship, because they should. But please don't misunderstand ... they should also challenge, contend, exhort, reprove, and admonish from the pulpit— this, the world will hate. For those who doubt this, read the writings of Paul, Peter, and James ... these men incited tremendous controversy, upset the entire religious system, and offended the world so much that it cost them their lives. The key, again, is to balance truth and love, mercy and repentance, and grace and holiness.

## Enter Compromise ... Exit Truth

Why so much compromise in the church? It's simple. When truth exits compromise enters. The church, in an attempt to relate to the world, has so popularized the ministry that it's hard to distinguish the church from the world (cf. 2 Thessalonians 2:10-12). I'm not suggesting that a church with a skate park or coffee house has replaced truth with gimmicks. A skate park and a coffee house may be a great idea. *What I am suggesting is that we have become a church that frowns on holiness and finds immorality and sexual perversion entertaining.* We spend very little time with God in prayer and reflection, and there's very little humility and brokenness. **As a result, the Holy Spirit is not guiding us—Hollywood is.**

Cancer begins with a single cell. In time, this tiny cell consumes the life of the body. The full-blown moral crisis that we are experiencing today began with small compromises. Again, times change, but God's standards do not. But you may say, "Everyone is doing it—what's the big deal?" If everyone's doing it, take a second look. "The masses are always wrong. In every generation the number of the righteous is small. Be sure you are among them" (Tozer). We can be "among them" by allowing the Holy Spirit to bless our work. The message and the messenger must both honor Him. (See Titus 2:7-8 for more on this.)

Although we want to relate to others, our lifestyle should reflect our core convictions. This doesn't mean that we should be prudish and judgmental, but real, humble, and loving. They'll know that we are Christians by our love and by our convictions, not by how well we imitate the world around us. I seldom hear non-Christians say, "I'm turned off by Christianity because Christians try not to compromise." But I do hear, "Christians who say one thing and do another really turn me off." **There's an enormous difference between witnessing and being a witness.** Guarding against compromise isn't just a good idea, it's absolutely necessary when it comes to preserving our testimony. Aside from guarding ourselves, you never know who might be watching. Again, a compromised life sends a compromised message. Proverbs 4:23 says that we should guard our heart because it affects everything we do. Everything? Yes, everything! I once heard Pastor John MacArthur say, "It's not about perfection, but direction." Is the direction of our heart toward God, or the world? Again, "Love not the world, neither the things that are in the world. If any man love the world, the love of the Father is not in him" (1 John 2:15 KJV), is not just a good suggestion, it's a powerful step of obedience that fosters spiritual growth.

Like the Old Testament prophet, Elijah, who spoke on God's behalf, the same plea goes out today, "How long will you falter between two opinions? If the LORD is God, follow Him" (1 Kings 18:21). Oswald Chambers offers this perspective about Jesus, "He never pleaded, He never entrapped; He made discipleship intensely narrow, and pointed out certain things which could never be in those who followed Him."[16] Chambers also said, "The words of the Lord hurt and offend until there is nothing left to hurt and offend. Jesus Christ has no tenderness whatever toward anything that is ultimately going to ruin a man in the service of God." To be the light we must live in the

**light.** *One reason why Christianity does not appeal to society is because society does not want the Christ that they see in many Christians.*

Throughout the Bible, we are commanded to remove anything that causes us to stumble—yes, anything. Again, this may sound as if it borders on legalism, and it can when taken to extremes. But when Paul addressed legalism in the second chapter of Colossians, for example, he zeroed in on festivals and Sabbath days, and on consuming or not consuming certain foods. Remember: there is a clear difference between legalism and wisdom—legalism is of no value against the lust of the flesh, but wisdom is. King David said, "I will walk within my house with a perfect heart. I will set nothing wicked before my eyes" (Psalm 101:2-3). Although he severely failed at times, David was saying that integrity and moral uprightness should be pursued, especially in the home. Being discerning has nothing to do with legalism; it has everything to do with spiritual integrity, wisdom, and moral purity. Colossians 3:17 declares that "whatever you do in word or deed, do all in the name of the Lord Jesus." Do all things to the glory of God.

The door of temptation swings both ways—we can enter or exit. The pull of sex, for example, is everywhere, and like a fishing lure, we don't notice the hook until we take the bait. Scan the TV and the Internet, view the covers of most magazines, listen to the radio, glance at the billboards that line our freeways and at the movies we view—sex surrounds us, and it's not getting any better. **Consequently, the more we feed this desire, the more we'll have to fight this desire.** Don't fight sexual desires; flee them (cf. 1 Corinthians 6:18).

Holiness is not a strange, outdated word. Holiness is being set apart or separated from anything that causes us to sin, whether mentally (in what we think) or physically (in what we do). Holiness begins in the heart. We should continually strive for holiness in all that we do and say. "The Holy Spirit is first of all a moral flame. It is not an accident of language that He is called the Holy Spirit, for whatever else the word holy may mean it does undoubtedly carry with it the idea of moral purity" (Tozer).

One youth pastor told me, "I don't worry about what I watch, or listen to, as long as my heart is right." But this is a very dangerous view. Most will admit, however, that this statement is really just an excuse to cross the line when it comes to entertainment. Let's be honest, we rationalize watching and listening to very questionable material because we enjoy it. This is nothing new. Throughout history, God's people turned from serving Him to worshipping gods associated with lust and sexual perversion. This preoccupation often meant the eventual destruction of the nation. "They became an abomination like the thing they loved" (Hosea 9:10). The good news, however, is that restoration often follows repentance. Of course I'm not suggesting that this youth pastor was worshipping false gods, but he was definitely making unwise entertainment choices that could eventually lead him away from God.

When it comes to entertainment, it's not about following rules. Let your freedom in Christ and a relationship with Him, guide you. We've all watched questionable material and have made wrong choices. Don't live with ongoing regret, but don't justify wrong behavior by thinking that God doesn't care about what you watch or listen to. He does care—we serve and love God with our mind (cf. Romans 7:25 and Luke 10:27). What we view and listen to clearly affects our relationship with Him. If we find dozens of hours a week to watch movies and television programs but have little time for God, our relationship with Him will suffer—period. Liberty has limits. The key is to ask, "Will it build me up spiritually, or pull me down?"

On the flip side, far too many of us have forgotten about grace. As a result, legalism surfaces. Legalism has been known to condemn all music, movies, and television programs that do not fit within pre-set boundaries. Legalism can be defined as a self-righteous attitude that rates spirituality by how well a person follows rules. A legalist often has a sliding scale mentality—the more rules and regulations a person follows, the more spiritual he or she becomes. The legalist often forgets that we are saved because of what Christ did, not by what we do or don't do. He or she may have the tendency to view struggling Christians as counterfeits because they don't measure up to a certain standard. Most Christians will struggle with legalism from time-to-time, and that's why it's important to discuss it and avoid it.

It's been said that grace is one of the most misunderstood of all Christian doctrines. If grace is abused, a person may continue in sin and see nothing wrong with it. If grace is neglected, one may never experience true freedom in Christ. Chuck Swindoll stated it this way, "The liberating truth about our freedom in Christ flies in the face of do-it-yourself religion and challenges Christ's followers who are enslaved to man-made rules and regulations to break free." He adds, "At the same time, grace promotes a powerful devotion to Christ and obedience to His Word, not to someone's guilt-giving list...".[17] Some matters must be determined by an individual's own conscience (cf. Romans 14:1-15), but some are crystal clear...what we put in our mind, for example, should honor God. We must learn to recognize what glorifies Christ and what clearly does not, and then choose accordingly. **Grace does not relieve us of responsibility. We actually live under a higher standard when grace, not rules, guides our decisions.** We who are living under grace should not want to continue in sin. We are free to choose what we allow to enter into our minds—but if it begins to control us, we are no longer free but bound. Compromise often begins with the first step in the wrong direction (cf. 1 Corinthians 10:23).

Let me leave you with this thought again: if you are a young adult, are you willing to do what it takes to protect your mind and your relationship with the Lord? If you are a pastor or leader, are you willing to do what it takes to protect your congregation against compromise? If you are a parent, are you willing to do what it takes to protect your family? It's your choice.

# EBook Sermon Links:

1. The Marketing of Evil: http://vimeo.com/68139775

2. The Cost of Carnality: http://vimeo.com/70891400

3. The Price of Pleasure: http://vimeo.com/60391744

# CHAPTER FOUR: Group Study Questions

1. "Light and darkness, right and wrong, good and evil, truth and error are incompatibles... when they compromise it is the light, the right, the good, and the truth that are damaged." Comment.

2. Before asking if an event, website, promotional idea, or advertisement is "culturally relevant," we should ask does it glorify Christ? Do you agree, or disagree? Explain.

3. Comment on this statement: *If we spend little time with God in prayer and in reading and following His Word, the Holy Spirit is not guiding us, Hollywood is.* How can a person change course?

4. Comment on this as well: Liberty has limits—the key is to ask, "Will it build me up spiritually or pull me down?" List ways that you can be built up.

5. List ways that Christians can relate to and serve the culture (missional), but, at the same time, promote truth (Romans 12:1-2)? Why is this challenging?

CHAPTER FIVE: *Desperate for Leadership*
*(for men)*

# Life is a Battleground, Not a Playground

"I won't watch my kids be physically abused anymore. I won't listen to my girls be called vile, vulgar names. I won't have things smashed or broken in the house. I won't get into a vehicle and listen to him rage. No more 'spending time together' with him sitting two feet away running pornography on the computer! I never believed in divorce so I just keep trying. I can no longer bear it. I'm not dying inside, I have died."

*-Email correspondence from a desperate wife and mother*

As a child, I was captured by the stories that my grandfather told about life on the farm in Oklahoma in the early to mid 1900s. The images I've held are not those of pleasant surroundings and ideal conditions; they are impressions of twelve-hour days spent working the land, dust storms that could devastate a crop, blistered and sunburned skin, and poverty unlike most Americans know today. Life, in general, was harder then, but interestingly enough, character seemed much stronger—it was a time when commitment, integrity, and honesty stood in place of contracts, disclosures, and bylaws. A handshake and a man's word were generally good enough. I'm not suggesting that we return to that time in history, but that we learn from the past and strongly encourage those same character traits today.

To carry the weight of responsibility as husbands, leaders, and fathers we must be *Desperate for More of God*. Unmistakably, the foundation we build today provides the strength that weathers the storm tomorrow. It's unfortunate that society focuses largely on external factors such as money, position, status, and recognition. These superficial values have left our nation in a moral, as well as a spiritual crisis. I recall an article written in celebration of Michael Jordan's 50th birthday by ESPN's senior writer Wright Thompson. He spent some time with M.J. and portrayed Jordan as very unhappy. "I would give up everything now to go back and play the game of basketball," Jordan laments. When asked how he copes with the devastating fact that he will never be who he was, Jordan states, "You don't. You learn to live with it." Thompson concludes, "The man has left the court, but the addictions won't leave the man."[18] **We've become a society focused on prosperity instead of provision, we value wealth instead of wisdom, and we are drawn to charisma instead of character.** Our foundation has slowly deteriorated, but that can be changed if we once again focus on God's Word and biblical principles.

Why a chapter primarily for men? Simple ... we are in desperate need of genuine leadership—broken, humble men—men who are not afraid to admit that they need God; men who are more worried about prayer than about status and recognition; men who petition God rather than position themselves. The state of the family today is disheartening. Men have largely forsaken their God-given role as spiritual leaders in their homes ... that, no one can deny. For example:

- Daily Bible reading and prayer are called fanatical while working twelve hours a day is called success.
- We build our career and neglect our marriage.
- Corporate executives are praised and family men frowned upon.
- We've increased our wealth but decreased our values.
- We search the heavens for answers and turn from the One who created them.
- Pride is considered an asset and humility a liability.
- We know more about our favorite athletes than our wives and our children.
- We'd rather be seen leaving a bar than leaving a church.
- We raise our hands and praise our favorite team yet fall asleep in church.

Men, begin by leading your family in the fear and admonition of the Lord. If you're single, begin developing godly character now (cf. 1 Timothy). You don't simply say, "I do," and become a man of character. The journey of leadership begins with the first step in the right direction. You must be *Desperate for More*.

You're not called to be a passive, weak, indecisive partner—you're called to protect, lead, and guard your family. You are to initiate prayer, defend your wife, shepherd your children, and make your home a holy sanctuary not a breeding ground for Satan. You're called to fight the enemy, not flee from him.

We are tired of weak, passive men who never contend, stand, or fight for anything worth dying for. Our nation is looking for character, our wives are looking for leaders, and our kids are looking for fathers. Men, STOP the silly video games, get off Facebook, kill your porn habit, tell your ungodly friends to hit the road. You're called to lead, love, and die, if necessary, for your family.

We are the reason that the nation is deteriorating. We are the reason the family is breaking down. We must stop blaming everything from God to the government; we are the stench in the nostrils of a righteous, holy, pure God. Men ... wake up! Life is a battleground, not a play ground!

I can hear it now, "Shane, you're being too hard on the guys. Back off." Step into my world for a moment. Recall the excerpt of an email that I received that opened this chapter. Sadly, this is not an isolated situation; it's happening every day. Re-read it and tell me if this message is too strong.

**Men who are hurting their families don't need to be encouraged and coddled; they often need to be confronted and challenged.** Then encouragement can take place. *Change is difficult if we always encourage but rarely challenge; coddle but not confront.* While concluding this chapter, the man referred to in the opening email was lovingly confronted and is now working toward reconciliation. I've had the pleasure of seeing Christ renew his marriage. What an incredible testimony!

Years ago, I stumbled across a journal entry from my wife that broke my heart, but first I felt betrayed and angry. She wrote, "I married a man who doesn't care about my dreams and goals in life. I've learned to live with this since separation isn't an option, but I will not allow him to do this to our kids." I was angry because the truth hurt, but after a long drive I began to realize that she was right. I was a controlling man with no regard for the dreams, ambitions, and goals of my family. Granted, I was not mean-spirited about their dreams, but I was controlling. I felt terrible and asked for forgiveness. I was breaking the spirit of my family because of pride and how things would make me look. That experience was a turning point. I now try to encourage my family versus discourage. I'm sharing this to illustrate the fact that God often uses confrontation and exposure to break us.

While dads jockey for position, build reputations, chase careers, and so on, its often mothers who pray, petition, nurture, care for, and lead. Granted, there are men who, through no fault of their own, experience failure in their home, but for the large majority, there is a critical need for spiritual leadership. Repentance is the first step. Knowledge is *knowing* that we need to repent, but wisdom is doing it. The power in the Word of God is found in the application. James 1:22 reminds us that we can deceive ourselves if we "know" what to do but fail to do it. Are you living in deception ... knowing but not doing?

# "How To" isn't the Problem

"I've had enough! I'm filing for divorce! You will never change," yelled the once loving wife as the door slammed behind her. Sadly, this scenario happens all too often. Change is difficult, but we risk endless difficulties and often tragedies if we don't change. Change requires self-examination, grace, responsibility, humility, discipline, and obedience ... character qualities that run counter-cultural. We have enough books and sermons on change to fill countless libraries—our problem isn't with "how to"; it's with "want to."

I vividly remember a men's conference where I spoke on the dangers of pornography. A man approached me after the message. His eyes were filled with tears when he said, "My wife is leaving me because of porn. This conference is my last chance." After talking and praying, we isolated that his desire was being fed primarily through ESPN. Many of the explicit commercials, along with the cheerleaders and the photos, sparked lust. After a few minutes, I said, "In addition to repentance, accountability, and transparency, remove the television and disconnect the Internet for a while. Show your wife that your marriage is worth more." His response was alarming, but characteristic of many men today, "I can't do that ... I'm a sports fanatic."

Surprised and disappointed, I asked, "How badly do you want it? How bad do you want a healthy marriage and a vibrant relationship with the Lord? How bad do you want the abundant life that Christ spoke of? How bad do you want to be a godly role model to your kids? Obviously, not bad enough." I ask the same question today, "How bad do you want it?" It all starts here. You must be *Desperate for Change.*

**1. Self-examination recognizes areas that require change.** Jesus often asked, "Do you want to be made well?" (cf. John 5:6). Although theologians are divided on the motive behind such questioning, one thought is clear: we must "want" to change, not just talk about it. Take anger for example, it does not produce good fruit (cf. James 1:20). What about controlling the tongue? The Lord hates gossip, backbiting, slander, etc. What about wrong attitudes? Self-righteousness and judgmentalism are very dangerous. What about addictions? This can include anything from foods to pills to drinks, and from pornography to other unhealthy lusts. Sadly, many do not want to change. If the truth be told, we enjoy sin.

One of the first steps toward change is in recognizing and admitting destructive areas. C.H. Spurgeon rightly noted, "We are never, never so much in danger of being proud as when we think we are humble." When challenging men in this area, I often ask, "Are you genuinely sorry and repentant, or are you just sorry that your reputation and life are on the verge of being ruined?" The difference between sorrow and repentance is vital because many confuse the two. It's possible to be sorry about the "consequences," but not truly repentant. A penitent person turns from sin—anger, for example, subsides, not remains. They accept full responsibility for their actions without blame, resentment, or bitterness. When repentance is genuine, we want to be reconciled with those we've injured. We seek forgiveness without conditions and stipulations. We take full (not partial) responsibility for our actions. We don't say, "But this and that...". There can be no "but's" when repentance is genuine. "I am sorry. I was wrong. Please forgive me," are often (although not always) healing words and signs of repentance. If this is not occurring, repentance has not taken place. Excuses need to stop before change and restoration can occur.

*2. True Repentance must take place.* Some suggest that repentance is self-improvement or a call to fulfill our natural potential. When we repent we do improve, and our God-given potential becomes more apparent, but repentance is not about self-improvement—it's about renouncing and turning from sin. Repentance is a change of mind that leads to a change in action ... brokenness, genuine sorrow over sin, and humility are marks of sincere repentance. Lasting hope and joy are also by-products of a right relationship with God, beginning with repentance. There is always a link between genuine change and sincere repentance.

On numerous occasions when I have spoken about the dangerous of sexual sin from the pulpit or during counseling, most enthusiastically agree that it's wrong, but continue anyway ("hear" but do not "do"). They are deceived according to James 1:22. Sexual sin is deceptive ... it draws us in to a false sense of attraction. Lust is extremely strong and enticing. It affects emotions, feelings, and our will at a very deep level. For those who are married, it has led to those devastating words due to adultery, "I don't love you anymore." At this point, unable to perceive and obey spiritual truth, sin's deception has taken over and spiritual blindness has set in. When sexual sin has gained a stronghold, the heart hardens and an array of excuses follows. **The spouse they once loved and cherished is now despised and discarded.** Sin continues to deceive with the ultimate goal of killing the marriage: "Sin when it is fully grown brings forth death" (James 1:15).

Obedience is crucial ... it stops sin dead in its tracks. Often, the only way out of adulterous and destructive relationships is to do what is right regardless of feelings. Feelings often deceive, but obedience can be trusted. Sadly, many do not experience freedom and true restoration because wholeness is found in obeying the truth, not just in hearing it. Church, for some, serves as therapy for this very reason. They hear about sin, are convicted, and leave feeling justified because they "heard" and "felt," but they did not repent and change. Or the opposite occurs ... they never hear about sin so change through repentance does not occur.

James 2:14 says, "What does it profit, my brethren, if someone says he has faith but does not have works ... faith by itself, if it does not have works, is dead." Scripture does not promote a works-based religion; it demonstrates the importance of having a genuine relationship with Christ that, in return, seeks to honor God and others through obedience. Genuine faith is reflected in obedience to God and His Word. The fruit that follows is sincere humility, selfless love, true repentance, and disengagement from the things of the world versus a love for them. Does your life reflect these characteristics? As you can see, hearing and obeying the truth are vitally important.

As a word of encouragement to those who have failed: if you feel discouraged, don't be! You can get back on track. Often, you'll have two choices—to fall backward or to fall forward. If you choose to fall forward into forgiveness, in time, God's grace will heal and restore you.

As a word of encouragement to single men: develop humility and godly character now so they can strengthen future relationships.

As a word of encouragement to those whose fathers may have failed them: God has given us the freedom to choose, and, in relationships, the choices of one can greatly affect the life of the other. But God can honor and bless your circumstance if you trust Him and forgive others. He can rebuild your life and open doors you might not have thought possible. Meanwhile, continue to pray and contend for the restoration of the relationship.

## The Power of Porn

The words, "By 2020, most women will be marrying men severely addicted to pornography," jumped out as I glanced through recent statements on pornography. If you have children, that statement should send shivers down your spine.

What was defined as pornography a few decades ago now fills our television screens on a nightly basis. We are being swept away by a culture that glamorizes porn ... we are a nation sinking in a vile and toxic cesspool. As men, we must fight this battle head on. Sexual purity isn't an option; it affects all areas of life. I estimate that pornography is an issue in eighty percent of the men that I've counseled with concerns to rage, abuse, and anger. These are all interwoven.

If a man is disciplined in the area of purity, chances are that he'll be disciplined in other areas. Discipline is a key ingredient of change. Leadership that is *Desperate for More of God* seeks to be disciplined and committed to the things of God, beginning with purity. However, discipline alone is not enough … only the power of God can radically set a man free. Sanctification is God's job, but obedience is ours, and is well stated in the phrase, "I'm a work in progress." Salvation is instantaneous, but sanctification is a process. One problem is that many men do not truly want victory badly enough.

Recall the men's conference where I spoke on the dangers of pornography. A man approached me about his struggle, "My wife is leaving because of porn. This conference is my last chance." As stated earlier, his response is not uncharacteristic of many men today, "I can't do that … I'm a sports fanatic." This is exactly why we are not seeing much change in this area. Overall, men do not want to take the necessary steps. They're often sad that they got caught, but rarely are they repentant. **Like an addict talking another hit, porn promises but never delivers.**

I have no idea whatever became of that man, but I do know that a half-hearted approach will not work. Pornography must be dealt with passionately and decisively. A favorite tool of the enemy, and a very destructive force against change, is the phrase, "I'll start tomorrow." **A man after God's heart immediately puts procrastination in the crosshairs and pulls the trigger.**

Pornography shouldn't be glamorized; it has to be taken seriously because most men struggle with it. It destroys marriages, godly character, and our relationship with the Lord. It is used by the enemy to kill, steal, and destroy. 1 Corinthians 6:9 warns us not to be deceived— the sexually immoral will not inherit the kingdom of God. Jesus adds, "But I say to you that whoever looks at a woman to lust for her has already committed adultery with her in his heart" (Matthew 5:28). Viewing pornography is either adultery (if married), or fornication (if single).

Sadly, teens and adults are becoming addicted to pornography at alarming rates. Pornography is considered free speech and has become one of the most lucrative businesses in America. Not surprising, it's often a major influence in the lives of those who commit sex crimes. It stands as a root cause of many divorces and many broken marriages. It plagues our churches and has become an epidemic. It's difficult to understand why one would attempt to defend it, let alone dabble in it.

Sex is good and God-given. It makes sense that God would create one act that distinguishes marriage from all other relationships; one that binds and holds the marriage relationship together. A marriage that is firmly anchored creates a stable environment in which to raise children and sustain commitment. Sexual intimacy was not created to be a recreational sport, it was intended as a spiritual bond to assure that "the two shall become one," and remain as one (Genesis 2:24). Pornography robs married couples of intimacy. The intimacy once shared is given to another. As time goes by, it's not uncommon for spouses to say, "I don't love you anymore"; failing to realize that love doesn't leave people, people leave love. True love is not an ecstatic, lustful feeling; it's a commitment...the foundation of marriage. Pornography destroys the very foundation on which marriage is built.

Some may view the following paragraphs as legalistic, but legalism reflects a self-righteous attitude. I'm not promoting that...I'm promoting wisdom. Wisdom reflects a heart committed to God's Word and moral purity. Obedience is a key ingredient when fighting the flesh. Even a quick view of the New Testament reveals that obedience is vital. We must avoid, remove, and dethrone— avoid places and people that trigger lust, remove the stumbling blocks, and dethrone the idol that has taken residency in the heart. I gave a two part message on this topic in 2013 entitled, *"god's at war."* I borrowed the title and some of the content from Pastor Kyle Idleman (no relation) who authored the book by the same title. (For those interested in hearing this message, visit WCFAV.org.)

The pull of sex is very strong; therefore, the pull away must be greater. There is nothing wrong with taking extreme measures. Jesus said, "If your right eye causes you to sin, pluck it out and cast it from you; for it is more profitable for you that one of your members perish, than for your whole body to be cast into hell. And if your right hand causes you to sin, cut it off and cast it from you..."

(Matthew 5:29-30). He is not advocating dismemberment since we can still lust and commit adultery in the heart even without an eye and a hand. He is saying that we must take necessary, often drastic, steps to avoid sin.

When I first set up accountability software on my computer that sent all websites visited to my wife's email every week, it made me very conscious of even seemingly innocent sites. It was, and is, a major deterrent. To some, this seemed extreme and unnecessary. Ironically, many of those who felt this way had a problem with porn. Conviction was propelling their jeers. **We cannot play with the lion that is sent to steal, kill, and destroy. He is an enemy not an inconvenience!**

As a word of encouragement to believers, Jesus has set you free—you do not have to be a slave to sin! Submit yourself to God and resist the devil; he must flee. Endure temptation as a good soldier. Deny the flesh and be filled with the Spirit. Do not yield to temptation or make provision for it; crucify it ... flee! Don't be brought under the power of temptation. God will make a way to escape that you may be able to bear it. These are all biblical commands when fighting sin. Unbridled sexual passions are perversions; they need to be crucified, not coddled: "Beloved, I urge you as sojourners and exiles to abstain from the passions of the flesh, which wage war against your soul" (1 Peter 2:11). The New American Commentary says this about the war of the soul:

> The depth of the struggle in which believers are engaged is explained by the words "which war against your soul." Obviously the desires of the flesh

that emerge in believers are quite strong if they are described in terms of warfare, as an enemy that attempts to conquer believers. Such desires must be resisted and conquered, and the image used implies that this is no easy matter. The Christian life is certainly not depicted as passive in which believers simply "let go and let God." The "soul" here does not refer to the immaterial part of human beings. The whole person is in view, showing that sinful desires, if they are allowed to triumph, ultimately destroy human beings.

Did you catch that? Sinful desires, if they are allowed to triumph, ultimately destroy. Those minimizing obedience in the Christian community should reconsider their position. Believers must resist, bear, endure, deny, fight, flee, and avoid temptation. Paul's words in 1 Corinthians 6:18 have been a tremendous help to me, "Flee sexual immorality. Every sin that a man does is outside the body, but he who commits sexual immorality sins against his own body." Flee means to "run away from danger." You don't contemplate, consider, or amuse the idea … you flee quickly.

On example that comes to mind is a pornographic magazine that I saw in the desert during my morning jog. As soon as I recognized it, I kept jogging and immediately sent my wife a text message. This transparency, accountability, and fleeing the scene immediately meant victory. Had I slowed my pace and began entertaining the idea, I could have lost this battle. Even searching for the words "fleeing sexual immorality" on my computer brought up many provocative sites. With danger just a click away, having my wife receive an email containing all the websites I visit is another great way of "fleeing." But please don't misunderstand, we all struggle. Don't idolize pastors or Christians leaders ... we struggle with the same issues. Look to Christ and Christ alone as your perfect example. **Men will always let you down; Christ will not.**

If you're single, find a mature believer of the same sex who can help hold you accountable. Accountability, by itself, doesn't work—it's not realistic to ask others to always hold you accountable. Your heart must be focused toward God and honoring Him. The accountability person simply complements and adds another level of security in the battle again sexual sin.

If you fall, fall forward into God's grace and forgiveness. This isn't a license to sin; its permission to call on God for forgiveness and restoration. As much as we need to be challenged, we also need to be encouraged. Obedience does not remove love, it helps to clarify it. Obedience is simply a by-product of God's faithfulness and love. I want to obey because of my loving relationship with Him.

## Purity isn't Optional

God's Word is clear and direct—sex is to be reserved to bring uniqueness to marriage alone. If couples experience sexual intimacy with one another before marriage, they will lose something that God had designed for them to share only as a married couple. Although your past may be tainted by sexual sin, God will honor your decision to abstain. This is not to say that couples who have failed to wait can't have a blessed marriage, but God wants to spare us the potential added pain of walking in disobedience.

As a word of hope, although our bodies cannot physically reverse the process of past sexual relationships, our mind and spirit can be renewed and restored. Don't allow past mistakes to cause future pain. *God is calling you back to a place of purity and wholeness; don't become discouraged and despondent because of past failure.* Recognize that those who have been forgiven much, love much (Luke 7:47). You can't change where you've been, but you can change where you're going. This new change in attitude and action is not only pleasing to God, but it will help you attract the "right" qualities in others as you pursue a lifelong partner.

When the Bible describes sin as a path that leads to death, it's not necessarily talking about physical death—although at times it is—it's describing separation from God; death can simply mean separation. Sexual sin resulted in the death of a family, a marriage, and the integrity of an individual. The entire family loses. Sin draws the life out of you and those closest to you. According to John 10:10, the enemy comes to steal, kill, and destroy; unwise choices and/or relationships promote destruction. Conversely, right choices and positive relationships promote health and growth. Consider your choices. And again, if you fall, fall forward!

References to sexual experiences in the Bible are often defined as "he knew his wife." To know, in this context, is to know intimately through sexual experience.

Regrettably, for those who experience sex before marriage, it is impossible to un-know what is known. Sexual experiences cannot be un-done. Each time we engage in premarital or illicit sex we add additional emotional weight to our lives, and it's very difficult to run a marital marathon while carrying the extra weight of sin. Weakness means the absence of strength, whereas meekness means strength under control. Those who refrain from illicit sex exhibit far more strength than those who don't. In essence, it takes more strength to say "no" than to say "yes." Isn't that the case in so many areas of life?

As men, we are called to be leaders in the relationship. Don't place the burden of leadership on the one you are dating; demonstrate self-control in the area of abstinence. When we demonstrate this type of discipline, we compliment her as someone of great value and respect. A word of caution to men and women: if the person who you are dating is not concerned with purity (despite your past), reconsider the relationship—if they are not concerned with doing what's right now, they may not be concerned about protecting you in other areas once married. Although a person may find you attractive, their motivation to protect purity should outweigh their desire for sex. If it doesn't ... you fill in the blank.

**If you've sinned in this area, you don't have to keep failing from this point forward—God will reward obedience**. There is hope and healing for those who desire it. Unmistakably, the quality of your choices today will affect the quality of your life tomorrow. If you desire a good marriage or a fulfilled single life in the future, it begins with the right choice today, followed by another right choice... and so on. For those who have chosen to postpone intimacy, it will be worth the wait. Ask yourself, "Do I want to experience the temporary pain of discipline or the nagging pain of regret?"

Let me restate my point: if you're currently involved in any type of sexual sin understand that it's not where God wants you to be. He cannot bless your decision to continue in a sexual relationship or pornography, but He can bless a decision to repent and abstain. Pre-marital sex (and porn) robs the couple of a level of intimacy and closeness reserved for life-long commitment. Sex should be enjoyed by a man and a woman the way God designed it—through an intimate, lasting, committed relationship (marriage).

Without a doubt, the largest factor contributing to the destruction of many relationships is the lack of sexual purity. Why then do so many continue to fall in this area? I vividly remember a story of a young boy who kept falling out of his bed. He finally asked his mother why he kept falling. She wisely answered, "It's because you don't stay far enough in." In the same way, many of us fall back into sin because we don't get far enough into God's framework of safety and protection.

Overcoming sin, especially sexual sin, can be a difficult battle for Christians, but purity is not optional, it's essential. In Romans 6 and 7, Paul has an open dialogue about our old sinful nature being crucified with Christ so that sin loses its power in our lives. Often, the good we want to do we do not do, and the evil we seek to avoid we sometimes practice. The result is misery, so Paul asks, "Who will free me from this body and life that are dominated by sin?" (cf. Romans 7:24). It leaves one to wonder, "If I'm dead to sin why is it still alive in me?" How can Paul declare that he is dead to sin in one verse, yet ask a few verses later "who will free me from the domination of sin in my life?" Romans 6:16 is the clarifying verse, "Whatever you choose to obey becomes your master?" We can choose sin, which leads to death, or we can choose to obey God. It's a choice, and once you make that choice it then makes you. Purity is not optional; it's essential.

How can we foster and encourage purity? Again, in review:

**Become men of prayer.** Men would live better if they prayed better. Porn cannot gain a stronghold in a broken, praying heart. Ten times out of ten, if a man is addicted to porn, he has no meaningful prayer life. If we're too busy to cultivate a prayer life that places God first—we're too busy. We're often too busy because we're doing too much. Again, "When faith ceases to pray, it ceases to live" (E.M. Bounds). We should never allow our relationship with God to suffer because we're too busy. Praying actually helps overcome addiction. It instills into our lives discipline, commitment, patience, peace, joy, and contentment—it fills us with the Spirit. We must spend much time on our knees before God if we are to overcome pornography and other addictions.

**Sorrow doesn't work; repentance does.** Many are sorry, even anguished about pornography and/or sexual sin, but not repentant. We must see sexual sin as God sees it—a sin that destroys—and repent from it. Repentance is not about self-improvement; it's about renouncing sin and turning from it. Repentance is a change of mind that leads to a change in action. Brokenness, genuine sorrow over sin, and humility are marks of sincere repentance. Most advice will fail if the heart is not changed. Repentance is the key.

*Avoid compromise.* The idol of sex is destroying our families, nation, and individuals. "If it feels good, do it," may be a great marketing slogan that promises fun and freedom but it brings disappointment and devastation. The enemy rarely pushes us off the cliff, so to speak. We're often led down one step at a time, one compromise at a time, one wrong choice at a time. For example, the enemy doesn't show a man the pain and anguish and the years of regret that pornography brings; he deceives him with the temporary enjoyment. If the full story was known beforehand (divorce, broken relationships with his children, distance from God, and so on) no doubt different choices might have been made. We're often not shown the pain that sin brings; we're enticed by the temporary pleasure. For example, Ariel Castro, who was exposed in 2013 for kidnapping three women and holding them for ten years, admitted that a deep addiction to pornography fed his perversion. He eventually committed suicide in prison. His idol promised pleasure but brought death and destruction. Sin brings death.

*Avoid looking intentionally at things that stimulate lust.* There are times when we cannot avoid what we see: a person walking by, a commercial on TV, or an unannounced Internet page that suddenly emerges. Temptation is not sin, but what we do with it can be. What we choose to look at determines where our thoughts will go. Determine beforehand to avoid looking at things that can stimulate lust. Deliverance is a heart issue, and it often involves action on our part. Again, sanctification is God's job, but obedience is ours. This is where the phrase "I'm a work in progress" comes from. Salvation is instantaneous, but sanctification is a process. David said, "I will walk within my house with a perfect heart. I will set nothing wicked before my eyes" (Psalm 101:2-3). Although he failed at times, David was saying that integrity and moral uprightness should be pursued, especially in the home. As men we must fight this battle, and often, the best way to fight is to flee.

***Avoid places that stimulate lust.*** I was impressed with an article about a man who avoided the beach in the summer after admitting his addiction to pornography to his wife. He concluded that being around women who were barely covered often triggered his compulsion (most men can relate). Another case involved a man who stopped visiting certain sections at a local bookstore, and another who avoided the gym at peak hours; both concluded that these things were stimulating lust. Although these examples may seem extreme, to counter lust, we must avoid places, people, or things that stimulate that desire. The gym, for example, is froth with enticement—barely covered women, tight this and low that—making it very difficult for men who truly desire purity. We must be very careful on Facebook as well. I know of marriages that have ended in divorce because of social media connections. Guys are very visual and the distractions can be endless. Additionally, if your trigger is when you're alone at home or work, consider texting your spouse or someone else acknowledging that you're struggling. You'll be amazed at how quickly the temptation leaves once it is exposed … exposure is a great deterrent. *What grows in the dark is killed in the light.* Pornography grows in the darkness of deceit and manipulation. We must come clean if we are trapped. Will it hurt initially? Yes, but the pain of obedience far outweighs the pain of regret. Sleeping on the couch for a few nights is no comparison to divorce court, and there are times when it may not be so easily forgiven. Regardless, you can never go wrong by doing what is right.

***What about accountability?*** Finally, enlist an accountability partner, but don't place all your hope in him. Accountability can be over-rated. Sexual sin is deceptive. Porn addicts will easily lie and deceive those holding them accountable. A person should not "hold you accountable"; the Holy Spirit should. Although accountability is good and recommended, it will not help if that's all you have. For example, those who download accountability software often find ways around it if their heart is not being changed. Consider having all the websites you visit emailed to your wife, or an accountability person on a weekly basis. Wisdom is needed here—maybe a spouse isn't the right person initially. But this type of accountability will severely hinder temptation and aid in transparency. Some may say, "I'm not willing to do that!" Why are they not willing to do that? It's often because they are not that serious about overcoming porn. Those who are serious will take the necessary precautions. Again, how badly do you want it? Are you truly *Desperate for More of God?*

As a word of encouragement to those who keep falling in this area: you're not alone; it's a struggle for most men. Follow the Apostle Paul's advice, "Forgetting those things which are behind and reaching forward to those things which are ahead" (Philippians 3:13). Forget your past mistakes, but remember the lessons learned because of them. Begin anew today and allow deep repentance to take place. Don't let discouragement and failure fuel the addiction. Sexual purity is not about perfection ... it's about repentance and truly seeking hard after God.

## Adultery—God Can Restore if Repentance Occurs

The Bible describes the intoxicating power of passion associated with lust and adultery. Misdirected passion deceives, misleads, and influences ... we walk in darkness, stumbling ... unable to see what we stumble over. This description well explains why so many caught in sexual sin describe a sense of confusion and a disconnect from God. Imagine walking through a cluttered room in pitch darkness. You stumble without knowing what you stumble over. This is a picture of the confusion and "stumbling" that accompanies sin. Adultery moves us from the altar to the courtroom—transforming a couple, once deeply in love, into bitter enemies. Hopes and dreams for the birth of a child, now twisted, become a nightmare for innocent children.

**How sad that sexual appetites often devour our own children, as well as ourselves.** Proverbs 9:17-18 describes adultery, "Stolen water is sweet, and bread eaten in secret is pleasant. But he does not know that the dead are there, that her guests are in the depths of hell." Adultery is selfishness. Many men fail to realize that pornography is adultery. Again, Jesus said that "whoever looks at a woman to lust for her has already committed adultery with her in his heart" (Matthew 5:28). Adultery hardens the heart toward spouses. Those who were once loved and cherished now feel insignificant and discarded. Children often feel to blame for not being good enough … trying hard enough. God help our selfish hearts! It would seem, that for loving parents, the thought of this horror would bring sexual sin to a sobering halt. Often, the only way out of adulterous and destructive relationships is to do what is right regardless of feelings. Feelings can be unstable and deceptive, but obedience to scriptural truths can be trusted.

The pain of adultery can make us bitter, or it can make us better—ultimately, it's our choice. God can restore if we are willing to admit that we were wrong. True repentance is unconditional and takes full responsibility for wrongs done. A truly repentant person is desperate to be forgiven … to focus on what he has done rather than placing blame or responsibility on others. Don't misunderstand, both spouses have work to do, but this comes later. There are primarily two areas that often prevent reconciliation:

**1. *Complete separation never occurs.*** Reconciliation is nearly impossible if complete separation does not occur between the couple involved in adultery, or with the pornography that is destroying the relationship. In the case of physical adultery, the spouse often feels that this new person makes him feel loved and appreciated, and that may be true, but so did his spouse when they first met. The type of love that God calls us to have does not leave people— people leave it. Deception lies in the fact that we often do not see the full effect of an affair until the sin is fully grown. Unrepentant sin brings death to the restoration process... death to clarity, direction, and peace (cf. James 1:14-15). Sexual sin hardens the heart and closes off forgiveness and brokenness. Again, when we are caught in sin, we are in darkness and we cannot see the things we stumble over. This deception blurs spiritual vision to see truth. As a result, we believe that God will turn a blind eye or be unconcerned. Worse yet, some even believe that God directed them to the adulterous relationship. Completely stepping out of the other person's life to see where God will lead is the only way to clear vision. I often wonder how many marriages are never restored simply because of pride and disobedience. Many "say" that they will stop communicating with the other person, but the truth is that they are afraid to lose the relationship—it's often a back up plan. The adulterer is often more concerned about the feelings of the other person, rather than the feelings of his spouse and family. At this point, he is often no longer attracted to the spouse—this false perception leads him back to the deceptive relationship.

*2. Genuine repentance does not occur.* This point of genuine repentance bears repeating even though we have covered it numerous times thus far. Many are sorry about adultery, but being sorry is not enough... only genuine repentance opens the ears of God and the restoration process. Many are sorry that they got caught; sorry that their

132

reputation and life are ruined, and so on. The difference between sorrow and repentance is vital because the two can be easily confused. It's not about "being caught," it's about "coming clean" and reversing direction (repentance).

It's possible to be sorry about the consequences of sin, but not truly repentant. A penitent person turns from his sin. They accept full responsibility without blame, resentment, or bitterness. When repentance is genuine, reconciling with those injured is a priority. Forgiveness is sought without conditions. We take full, not partial, responsibility for our actions. A truly broken and repentant person cannot continue in a relationship that he or she knows is wrong ... a relationship that is destroying the family. A person who is genuinely repentant will jump at the opportunity to foster restoration—he or she will walk away from the affair. Actions reveal the condition of the heart. (For those interested in learning more about genuine repentance, the message is available on our website and is entitled, *Hearing and Doing*.)

There is hope. Don't give up; look up. Those who are *Desperate for More of God* will focus on restoration. There are consequences for past mistakes, but the answer is to live in God's arms redeemed rather than to live broken outside of His will. Again, which way will you run?

## Unrighteous Anger—Explodes, Shatters, and Damages

The Bible clearly differentiates between righteous and unrighteous anger. Anger can be the correct response or a dangerous emotional reaction. The nature of anger is defined by the motive and the condition of the heart. Anger over issues that anger the Lord such as crime, abortion, pornography, abuse, oppression, and so on, is justifiable and can cause positive action. If anger sparks prayer and a Christ-like stance, it can be productive. Martin Luther said, "When I am angry, I can pray well and preach well."

The focus of this section will be on destructive anger. Prisons are at capacity because of anger. Men and women rage at their children because of anger. Families are destroyed because of anger: "Anger worketh not the righteousness of God" (James 1:20 KJV). We'll never walk fully in the will of God when anger continues unchecked and unguarded.

For most, the act of killing an unborn child is unthinkable, yet, the sad reality is that anger is killing our children relationally, emotionally, spiritually, and, in some cases, physically. Josh McDowell once stated that the reason so many young people are losing ground in the area of spiritual truth is because their parents are providing poor examples. His words should pierce every parent's heart, "One of the most common questions I get from young adults is, 'How could we live for Christ, when we don't want the Christ that our parents have?'"[19]

Anger causes children and spouses to walk on eggshells. They live in fear of triggering a volcano of angry emotions. Children and spouses should feel safe and secure in their own home. Home should be a safe-haven and a shelter. God makes no excuses for anger; nor should we. It doesn't matter how we were raised, what we've been through, our circumstances, or why we are this way, we must repent of this deceptive sin.

Anger can also prevent or hinder Christian leadership. According to Titus and 1 Timothy, elders, pastors, and leaders must not be angry, short tempered, or hot-headed, but rather, gentle and kind...not easily angered. Additionally, although a wife cannot qualify a man for pastoral leadership, she may disqualify him indirectly if anger is an issue in her own life.

Moses was not able to enter the Promised Land because of anger. Jacob cursed two of his sons because they were hot-headed men. David, because of anger and adultery, had Uriah killed in battle. Saul became enraged at David's promotion and sought to kill him. Anger is not a little character flaw; it's a deadly flame that fuels a raging fire that consume everything in its path. History is filled with angry men and women who derailed their destiny. Do we, then, believe that we are exempt from the consequences of anger?

Anger is often a secondary, not primary, emotion; it's a by-product of sinful attitudes. In order to better combat anger, one must deal with the root cause. This is why many never harness anger—they are trying to "be better" rather than starve the source that flames the anger. With that said, let's briefly examine a few primary causes that fuel anger:

- *Selfishness.* This can be defined as focusing on one's own advantage, pleasure, or well-being without regard for others. Selfishness fosters anger in adults the same way it does in children resulting in angry temper tantrums. They are manageable in four year olds, sad at 14, and embarrassing at 34. James 3:16 states that where envy and selfish ambition exist, you will also find disorder and every evil practice, including anger. Self-centeredness is closely related to pride. When we believe that our needs are more important than the needs of others, and we think more highly of ourselves than we should, selfishness begins to fuel anger when things don't go as planned. Jesus humbled Himself to the point of death, even death on a cross. He asks us to humble ourselves in our daily lives as well. Humble people aren't easily angered. Conversely, prideful, arrogant people are. Don't get me wrong, I have not mastered this area. I am a prideful man working on humility on a daily basis.

Luke 14:11 (KJV) states, "For whosoever exalteth himself shall be abased; and he that humbleth himself shall be exalted." Abase means to degrade, belittle, or humiliate. How many times do we feel degraded after an angry, selfish outburst? How about belittled or humiliated? Pride causes us to place more emphasize on things than people. A popular saying bears repeating, "We are to love people and use things." Today, we tend to love things and use people. Pride causes us to take pleasure in the things of the world rather than the things of God. For instance, husbands and wives don't marry filled with love and passion one day only to lose it the next. Marriage slowly deteriorates because more attention is given to self than spouse.

- *Jealousy fuels anger.* We are prone to jealousy—neighbors can be jealous of neighbors, churches jealous of successful churches, businessmen of other businessmen, and so on. We can offset jealously which leads to anger by rejoicing in positions and promotions of others; be glad when the Lord blesses them. James 3:14-15 says that bitter jealousy is not of God, but is earthly, unspiritual, and demonic. Not surprisingly, gossip springs from jealousy. But be encouraged, being tempted with jealously is not sin, caving into it is. Take wrong attitudes to God in prayer. Repent and ask for forgiveness.

- *Pride is the root cause of anger.* Selfishness is looking out for number one, whereas pride is thinking that we are number one. Selfishness and pride are closely related: "A proud and haughty man, 'scoffer' is his name; he acts with arrogant pride" (Proverbs 21:24). Pride is often a catalyst for criticism, division, and anger. It jeopardizes our health and the health of our family—spiritually, mentally, emotionally, relationally, and physically. Proverbs 18:21 reminds us, "Death and life are in the power of the tongue." Ask, "Are my words going to build others up or tear them down?" Angry words expressed to others can play an enormous role in shaping or reshaping their lives, especially when it comes to what we say to our spouse and children. A prideful person may not get this far along in the book, but if he does, I hope that he sees the deception of pride.

- ***Addiction fosters anger.*** Addiction controls, influences, and provokes anger. 1 Peter 2:11, "I urge you ... to abstain from the passions of the flesh, which wage war against your soul." Addiction can be packed in pills, porn, alcohol, food, and so on. Addiction, to alcohol, for example, often fuels angry temper tantrums and explosive outbursts. Addiction to caffeine often does the same; it's a powerful stimulant that fuels anger, irritability, and a quick temper (hot-headed). The *Diagnostic and Statistical Manual for Mental Disorders* lists caffeine-related disorders such as caffeine intoxication, caffeine-induced anxiety disorder, and caffeine-induced sleep disorder—all can lead to angry outbursts and extreme irritability. Don't rationalize and make excuses for addiction. By excusing actions, we deny responsibility. Take responsibility and make the needed changes. (More on this in the chapter on health.)

- ***Guilt—not doing what we know is right—often leads to anger.*** As we just discussed, those addicted to porn, gambling, alcohol, stimulants, and many other things are often angry people. Guilt and shame fuel the anger. I've been there. Proverbs 13:15 was a wake-up call for me: "The way of the transgressor" is hard. It's hard because we are fighting against God. But 1 John 1:9 offers hope, "If we confess our sins, he is faithful and just to forgive us our sins and to cleanse us from all unrighteousness." Acts 3:19 adds that repentance leads to times of refreshing. Repentance and obedience to God's Word frees us from shame and guilt, and can lessen anger.

Are there any areas in your life, such as anger, that you need to deal with? If so, I encourage you to seek forgiveness and repentance today. James 4:6 says that God gives grace to the humble but resists the proud. It's our choice.

## Help Wanted: Bold Men

There is a very troubling trend in the evangelical church—men, real men, are fading from the scene. Men were once bold, audacious, and driven (in a good way). Now passivity, fear, and laziness dominate the scene. Why are many failing to lead? In my opinion, the problem is two fold.

First, true conversion (surrender to the Lordship of Jesus Christ) is simply not occurring in the hearts of many claiming to be Christians. The reason some aren't leading is because they are not genuinely following Christ. Granted, most men struggle with leading, but there is something wrong when we don't even try... we give up before the battle begins. Martin Luther reminds us, "Where the battle rages, there the loyalty of the soldier is tested."

Second, brokenness and humility are missing. Often, we don't think of leaders as broken and humble. But the Bible clearly demonstrates that genuine leadership is shaped on the anvil of brokenness—from Moses to Paul—humility and brokenness are always characteristics of godly men. Remember, meekness is not the absence of strength; it's strength under control.

Leonard Ravenhill's son, David, tells of a time prior to his father's death when seminary students would request to see his father "for the sole purpose of having him lay hands upon them in order to receive his mantle." In the same way that Elijah passed his mantle/calling to Elisha, these students apparently desired the same. Leonard Ravenhill would simply respond, "Everyone wants to have my mantle, but nobody wants my sackcloth and ashes." His statement is profound—many want the recognition but not the brokenness; they want the honor but not the humility.

Again, we are in desperate need of broken, humble men—men who are not afraid to admit that they need God; men who are more worried about prayer than about status and recognition; men who "petition" God rather than "position" themselves; men who plead not posture, contend not complain. The great preacher, C.H. Spurgeon, once said, "I would rather teach one man to pray than ten men to preach." We have plenty of preachers but very few humble prayer-warriors.

Brokenness, true brokenness, is humiliating and painful, but it is the only way to truly be filled and led by the Spirit. An analogy that comes to mind is that of a shepherd. I'm not sure of the validity, but the principle applies. Perhaps you've heard, in times passed, that a shepherd might break the leg of a lamb that continually wandered from the flock, and thus, from the shepherd's protection. The shepherd would then splint the broken leg and carry the lamb on his shoulders for weeks until the leg healed. As painful as this was for the lamb, it was necessary to protect it from being ravished by wolves or other predators. In time, through the broken and dependant relationship, the lamb learned to walk and to remain in the protective presence of his shepherd.

What will it take to bring us back to the Shepherd? Death to self is a key ingredient. To be filled with the Spirit, we must be first emptied of pride and arrogance. Humility and brokenness allow His power to flow freely. In short, Spirit-filled believers make a difference. As Christians, we are given the Holy Spirit, but what we do with Him is largely up to us—we can quench and grieve Him, thus causing Him to withdraw, or we can truly surrender our life to His influence (cf. 1 Thessalonians 5:19; Ephesians 4:30). Often, the only thing standing between us and the work of the Holy Spirit is our will; hence the desperate need for humility and brokenness. The hammer of God must be allowed to break our will. The Holy Spirit will not empower you to do what you want to do, but He will empower you to do what God wants you to do. Pray for the Spirit's influence, desire it above all else, and continually live a life that glorifies Christ—*the Holy Spirit is given to those who obey God* (cf. Acts 5:32).

If you doubt the role of the Holy Spirit in the life of a Christian, simply read the New Testament Book of Acts. If God seems distant, Bible study boring, and church irrelevant, it's probably because the work of the Holy Spirit is being suppressed. More change will be seen outwardly as the Holy Spirit is given more power to rule inwardly.

Leonard Ravenhill, in his compelling book, *Revival Praying,* wrote: "Since something is obviously stopping the Spirit's inflow to us Christians, the same thing is stopping His outflow from us. With the Spirit's help we need to search for this hindrance." In my opinion, the hindrance is often pride. I sincerely believe that the greatest need in the lives of Christians today is to remove pride so that the power of the Holy Spirit can flow through us. We can't be full of the Holy Spirit if we're full of ourselves. Sadly, the only thing holding many churches together is social activity, not the activity of the Spirit. It's been said that if Christianity today (as a whole) were a poison, it would harm no one, and if it were a medicine, it would cure no one. As incredible as this sounds, it may be true, at least to some degree. **When we ignore the truth, frown upon spiritual disciplines, and neglect the foundational doctrines of the Christian faith, we become powerless.**

So the question is, "Are you willing to be completely obedient to the Spirit and surrender your life to Him?" If so, it will require a rejection of the cultural mindset ... a total transformation of heart. The solution is to fill ourselves with the things of God. As He increases, we decrease. The desire to be filled with the truth of God's Word must be a priority. Every area of our life should be affected as we surrender to His influence. This is why some people are more sensitive to the things of God—they are filled with His Spirit.

Let us take a turn and briefly discuss the fear that is gripping our world. Many are concerned with the direction of our nation, and the government in particular.

I agree with many of the concerns, but the greater concern may be that we are allowing fear to paralyze and polarize. **A minimizing of sovereignty is directly related to a magnifying of worry.** "Most Christians salute the sovereignty of God but believe in the sovereignty of man" (R.C. Sproul). Many are prepared militarily but not spiritually. They are instilling unhealthy fear in their families ... putting the fear of man into them rather than the fear of God. Boldness also involves sheltering and protecting, not only our thoughts, but the thoughts and emotional well-being of our family.

I created a media firestorm early in 2013 when I said the following during a sermon, "I hear all about Glock, Smith & Wesson, and Remington, but little about brokenness, surrender to God, and humility. Our gun safes are full but our prayer closets are empty. We need to spend less time watching the news, and more time with Matthew, Mark, Luke, and John."

Most who responded got it, but some completely missed the heart of the message. Are we called to protect our families spiritually, emotionally, and financially, but not physically? Of course not, but our trust must be in God and God alone. Every time God's people trusted in their weapons, military strength, and armies, He called them to repentance. Our protection is in our daily submission to Him. Psalm 121:2 adds, "Where does my help come from? My help comes from the Lord, the Maker of heaven and earth. He will not let your foot slip—he who watches over you will not slumber...". **Our current fear trend beckons us to be very careful about who, or what, we "worship." Who, or what, we place our trust in.**

Please don't misunderstand, I am concerned with the overall direction of our nation and the family. I'm also concerned that we are watering down the gospel to make it more marketable. I'm concerned that people moreover, are having their ears tickled rather than having their lifestyles challenged. I'm concerned that they're hearing what they want to hear and not what they need to hear. I'm concerned that they're learning about blessings, love, and happiness, but not repentance, sin, and longsuffering. We're not living in the year 1517, and most of us are not in Wittenberg, Germany, but would be to God that another Martin Luther would nail a revised *95 Theses* to the church doors calling for prayer, humility, and repentance before God—turning us back to truth and away from fear—back to Christ and away from the broad road that leads to destruction.

In our day, where are the men who are more concerned about God's opinion than the opinions of others. Where are the men who care more about their spouse than their careers? Where are the men who choose time with their kids over time with their drinking buddies? Where are the men who share in the rearing of their kids rather than pass it on to someone else? Where are the men who lead their families in the fear of the Lord rather than cater to the culture? Where are the men who are hardworking and diligent rather than lazy and frivolous? Where are the men who weather the storm, battle the enemy, and guard their home? Granted, I appreciate those who are, but as a whole, the culture has programmed us in such a way that we are lacking. The one thing that all great Christian men have is the one thing that many are lacking—the power of the Holy Spirit. We need men of extraordinary prayer, brokenness, and humility. Men filled and clothed with power from on high. *The men who do the most for God are always men of prayer, boldness, fortitude, and perseverance.*

Here are some examples from the past to motivate: E.M. Bounds, who was born in 1835, began his three-hour prayer routine at 4am. To him, prayer was not a short prelude, but an empowering priority. Edward Payson, who ministered during the Second Great Awakening, was said to have worn grooves into his hardwood floor as a result of prayer. It was said of John Hyde who left for the mission field in 1892 that he would stay on his face before God until the answer came. William Bramwell, a powerful Methodist circuit rider, often spent hours a day on his knees until his death in 1818. Adonia Judson attributed his success in Burma as a missionary to a life of prayer; as did J. Hudson Taylor, founder of the China Inland Mission. George Mueller who never asked for a dime, petitioned God for millions of dollars to fund his orphanages in the 1800s. John Fletcher, one of the leaders of the Methodist movement, stained the walls of his room with the breath of his prayers until his death in 1785. "When faith ceases to pray, it ceases to live" (E.M. Bounds). When men cease to pray, they cease to live, really live for Christ.

Some are asking, "Wait a minute. Who has that much time to pray and truly seek God...we are all too busy?" You're right, but we are often too busy because we're doing too much. "We must spend much time on our knees before God if we are to continue in the power of the Holy Spirit" (R.A. Torrey). Additionally, you are called to pastor and shepherd your home. This is not the primary responsibility of the local church ... it's your responsibility. Our porn addicted, sex saturated, video game, lazy mentality must be challenged. Godly leadership runs counter-cultural.

If you truly want to foster boldness you must build intimacy with God. You'll have to remove lesser priorities from your life. Years ago, I realized that if I wanted to grow spiritually, some things would have to go, or at the very least, be minimized. I needed to reprioritize my life. Instead of watching hours of television a day, I began to devote my time to activities that strengthened my relationship with the Lord. I cannot begin to tell you how much of a difference that made. Although far from perfect, I began to put first things first. As a result, I began to hunger for God's Word and spiritual truth like never before. I learned that it's impossible to develop a deep respect and desire for God if we repeatedly fill our mind with things that oppose Him.

The depth of your relationship with God is in direct proportion to the depth of your commitment to Him—great commitment, great relationship—poor commitment, poor relationship. Prayer matters. *The prayer closet equips, anoints, and empowers.* It was said of Jesus, "No man ever spoke like this Man" (John 7:46). He had great authority, and spent much time in prayer. Mark 1:22 adds, "And they were astonished at His teaching: for he taught them as one that had authority, and not as the scribes." Luke 4:36 records, "For with authority and power He commanded the unclean spirits, and they come out." God-given boldness and prayer go hand-in-hand. You can't have one without the other.

## EBook Sermon Links:

1. Hindrances to Prayer: https://vimeo.com/76941316

2. Help! My Plan isn't Working: https://vimeo.com/57997410

3. Whoever Loves Discipline, Loves Knowledge: https://vimeo.com/54923603

4. Words and Actions Reveal the Heart: https://vimeo.com/53949414

5. Proverbs and Parenting: https://vimeo.com/55397777

## CHAPTER FIVE: Group Study Questions

1. Do you agree that men have largely forsaken their God-given role as spiritual leaders in their homes? If so, how can you be different?

2. We must "want" to change, not just talk about it. List two areas that you can begin changing today (cf. James 1:22).

3. Why is sexual purity so important? What are some practical steps that you can take to extinguish lust?

4. What does 1 Corinthians 10:13 mean to you? It states, "No temptation has overtaken you except such as is common to man; but God is faithful, who will not allow you to be tempted beyond what you are able, but with the temptation will also make the way of escape, that you may be able to bear it."

5. Are you willing to be completely obedient to the Spirit and surrender your life to Him? If so, how can you begin, or continue with, that journey today?

# Marriage—the Hammer of God

"My marriage is lifeless and cold. Where did the passion go? We live in the same house, but we barely know each other. I love him but I don't like him. Divorce never crossed my mind, but now the thought is a daily struggle."

*On-line listener*

"I'm leaving my husband and our two small children. I know what the Bible says, but God knows my heart and He just wants me to be happy."

*Mom and Housewife*

*"It's almost too late"* jumped from the pages as I read an article by noted author and speaker, Josh McDowell. He stated that the reason so many young people are losing ground in the area of spiritual truth is because their parents are not involved in teaching them in word or action. As stated in the last chapter, he said, "One of the most common questions I get is, 'How can we live for Christ, when we don't want the Christ that our parents have?'" Wow, that should force us all to ask, "Who am I influencing, and who's influencing me?" Now, more than

ever, it's time to make solid choices in unstable times. When the deterioration of the family is coming from within the same walls that were designed to protect it, it's time for change.

If you are a parent, or plan to be one, your greatest investment will be in your children—period! Your goal may be to own a business, climb the corporate ladder, or pursue a profession; whatever you choose, there is no greater opportunity than to promote the spiritual success of another, especially your child's. Proverbs 22:6 (NIV) reminds us, "Train a child in the way he should go, and when he is old he will not turn from it." **Character is not only taught; it's caught.** It's demonstrated through the lives of parents.

We live in a society that emphasizes wealth and possessions, but these things have no eternal value. I hardly remember my parents' income or many of the material things they gave me. I do, however, remember the values they taught, those things that money cannot buy. It's been well stated that the best things in life aren't things. Although I took a temporary detour in my younger years, my parents' example left a lasting impression. Never underestimate the power of parenting!

It's possible to succeed in business, but fail at home. Look around, it's happening everywhere, from the pulpit to the boardroom. Unfortunately, the price of success is often paid at the family's expense. A friend of mine once shared a tragic story. He told of a trip to the hospital to visit a man who was dying. The man could no longer speak; he could, however, write. What followed was more devastating. The man cried as he wrote that he regretted not spending more time with his family. He was in anguish over the fact that he had not been a better father and husband, but, instead, had built his life around other things. When all is said and done, it's devastating to find that life was invested in those things that hold no lasting value. Be grateful and consider it a privilege that God has given you the ability to make a difference in the life of another.

## Personal Opinions Vary—Truth Does Not

The hot topic of same-sex marriage and/or homosexuality cannot be simply glanced over in a chapter on marriage. To be *Desperate for More of God* means that we must have solid biblical convictions in this area as well.

I have nothing but compassion for those trapped in any type of sexual sin. Those who strongly believe in the Bible and God's will regarding sexual behavior also strongly believe in unconditional love and forgiveness. To say that authentic Christians hate or fear those trapped in the homosexual lifestyle demonstrates a gross misunderstanding of the Christian faith. To "confront in love" simply comes from a desire to honor God and to truly love and care for others. Warning, confronting, challenging, advising, and admonishing are all characteristic of genuine love. Parents warn, confront, challenge, and admonish daily. Truly misled or self-serving individuals would wrongly attribute these traits to "hate."

Let's be careful not to confuse hate-speech with loving confrontation, intolerance with biblical truth, and rights with sexual preferences. As we read in the first chapter, certain "rights" and "wrongs" called absolutes are given by God to save man from himself. This is why many Christians cannot condone same-sex marriage. **Those who embrace this lifestyle are often those who do not embrace God's absolutes—both cannot be true.** In the same way that a foundation supports the entire structure, house or skyscraper, foundational biblical truths support the social structure. Nearly all of our social issues are related to the stability and structure of the God-ordained family.

Ironically, as I was writing my last book, a postmodern leader made headlines by suggesting that those who embrace the homosexual lifestyle can live in harmony with biblical Christianity. Many say that we cannot take a position on homosexuality because all positions will hurt someone. Here's my question, "Are those who defend homosexuality, or who say nothing, truly loving the homosexual, or are they simply seeking to avoid conflict?" For instance, if they are more concerned about being liked and accepted than being truthful, do they really care for homosexuals more than those who are willing to risk their reputation, and quite possibly their safety, in order to speak the truth in love?

The answer is obvious: authentic Christians love the truth and others to the degree that they are willing to risk the consequences of confrontation in order to help others. This is genuine love, not hatred.

In 2013, an online viewer made the following comment to a friend, "When I watched the video, *Same-sex Attraction—Balancing Grace and Truth*, I was cut to the heart. I cried out to God to save me... and He did. I'm now trying to minister to my partner who is dying of AIDS." God used the balance of truth and grace in this sermon to convict, challenge, and change. The ability to relate to people on their level, show genuine concern, and love them regardless of their lifestyle is the mark of true Christianity—compassion without compromise. *(Ebook readers, click the following link to view this sermon: http://vimeo.com/47460132)*

Unfortunately, Christians often embrace one of two extremes. At one extreme are those who insult or who are violent toward those trapped in this lifestyle. Homosexuality appears at the top of their sin list. With this group, there is very little love or compassion. The other extreme excuses this sin and looks the other way. Both extremes are wrong and offer a false impression of genuine Christianity. **"When we become so tolerant that we lead people into mental fog and spiritual darkness, we are not acting like Christians—we are acting like cowards"** (A.W. Tozer).

## I Just Want to be Happy

From my experience, most walk away from their marriage commitment because of a false view of happiness. One example that stands out is that of a young woman who left her husband and small children. "I just want to be happy," was her reason. I'm not minimizing the need for a joy-filled marriage, but this excuse does not align with biblical truth; it aligns with self-deception. Look into the eyes of your child and tell them, "I'm sorry I'm leaving. I just want to be happy." Imagine the crushing blow a child must feel. But excuses are made such as, "They'll be fine ... they'll get over it ... kids are resilient; they'll bounce back." But that's not the case. Divorce leaves a mark that few ever break totally free of.

If you believe that freedom and/or a new relationship makes people happy, think again. Why do millionaires, movie stars, and top entertainers often turn to spirituality, drugs, and alcohol if new relationships satisfy? They discover that money and fame, and a new relationship are not the answers. Celebrities frequently admit being happy when their career produces fame and fortune but very unhappy when it doesn't. Many of us do the same thing— we often measure happiness by what's "happening" to us. When things go right, we're happy; when things go wrong, we're unhappy. If happiness is always measured by our circumstances, the road ahead is going to be very disappointing.

**When our godly desires are being fulfilled, joy is brought to our lives.** The goal, then, is to align our desires with God's. God wants us to experience a fulfilled and abundant life. Problems arise when we seek happiness outside of His will.

Most are familiar with the statistics on failed marriages; they are alarming. Divorce is an epidemic. Many kids are raised by just one parent. The very foundation of the family is collapsing more and more every day. But there is hope. The more I pastor the more I realize that marriage can be a wonderful sanctification tool if we allow the hammer of God to shape us. It's time to challenge men and women to step up ... to be what God has called them to be. It's time for the hammer of God to fall and crush pride, arrogance, and selfishness. I'm not pointing fingers. I'm a fellow pilgrim on this journey. These words hurt and pierce my heart as well ... and that's good. Conviction is a wonderful gift from God for those who become better instead of bitter. **When the hammer of God falls, self is shattered and God's will becomes clear.**

In the past, commitment was the factor that held the family together. It was in that setting that children learned, love grew, and character developed. Divorce was rarely an option. In general, a husband or wife was considered an asset not a liability. Today's high divorce rate is simply an indicator of how society has changed. I'm suggesting that we resurrect a servant's heart and a commitment to the marriage relationship. If pride, arrogance, and selfness are destroying, or have destroyed your marriage, it will take humility, servitude, and genuine love to rebuild ... to keep the course regardless of detours and setbacks.

Those who succeed in marriage walk through adversity, not without it. There's no best time to start. Simply start now and remember that as long as you take two steps forward, even after stepping back, you'll continue to move in the right direction. A healthy marriage is a by-product of those who are *Desperate for More of God.* **Hunger for God doesn't hinder marriage,**

**it helps it.** How can we truly be filled with the Spirit of God if we are full of ourselves? How can we truly know Him, and yet, neglect our marriage? We can't.

If one desires a great marriage, he or she needs to be a great spouse. If one desires a good job, he or she needs to be a good employee. If one desires a better relationship with his or her children, they need to be better parents. Despite what you might think, you do have the power to change according to God's Word. It's not the difficult circumstances of life that cause failure, but our attitude and response to the circumstances that determines whether we succeed or fail. Anger, resentment, bitterness, failure, frustration, and un-forgiveness can produce a negative, unproductive attitude!

Please don't misunderstand, I'm not discounting the deep emotional and psychological pain associated with failed or difficult marriages, nor am I suggesting that divorce is never an option, but I do want to remind you that God makes provision for all of our needs, beginning with our spiritual foundation. I also realize that this chapter will not cover all the dynamics of marriage. My goal is to point you to the One who has the answers... seek Him with all your heart, mind, soul, and strength. God often uses marriage to sanctify, challenge, and change, but we must allow the hammer of God to shape and chisel our character.

## How to Strengthen the Foundation

Throughout my teen years, I worked with my father in the under-ground construction business. My dad's closest

156

friends, builders respected for their work, were very careful in preparing the ground and laying the foundation. Granted, the cost to build a strong foundation was expensive, but a weak foundation would cost more. Without proper support, a structure may not be sound and could present future problems.

Developers hired architects and engineers, appointed a contractor, paid fees to the county or to the city, as well as to other departments; developed a set of plans, and used heavy equipment to move tons of dirt, all to prepare the foundation. If only we were as careful in preparing for marriage and sustaining our marriage. In the same way, a relationship with Christ provides the foundation for strong marriages. The foundation built today provides the strength to weather the storm tomorrow. In Matthew 7:24-27, Jesus said, "Therefore whoever hears these sayings of Mine, and does them, I will liken him to a wise man who built his house on the rock: and the rain descended, the floods came, and the winds blew and beat on that house; and it did not fall, for it was founded on the rock. But everyone who hears these sayings of Mine, and does not do them, will be like a foolish man who built his house on the sand: and the rain descended, the floods came, and the winds blew and beat on that house; and it fell. And great was its fall."

This Scripture should cause all Christians to search their hearts as to whether they are truly obeying God in all areas of life. It's unfortunate that today's marriages focus primarily on external factors (e.g., looks, money, position, status, keeping up with the Jones', etc.). These superficial values have left marriage in a moral, as well as a spiritual crisis. We've become a society focused on prosperity instead of provision, we value wealth instead of wisdom, and we are drawn to charisma instead of character. It's little wonder that divorce is at an all-time high—our foundation has slowly deteriorated.

Marriage today is not failing because it's more difficult than in years past—it's failing because the foundation has weakened. A "genuine" relationship with Christ is the only solid rock on which marriage must be built. Sadly, most are neglecting their foundation. Do you have a genuine relationship with Christ, or are you simply going through the motions? Again, it all begins here.

Recent research shows that many married couples who are unhappily married but who stay together may actually be happier years later. The opposite is often true for those divorced. Although those who divorce may temporarily escape the pain, divorce introduces new emotional and relational difficulties. In a nutshell, unless it is severe and/or life threatening, weather the storm—it's worth it. Though the road ahead may be uncertain at times, the solid foundation beneath will never shift.

A few brief decades ago, being a devoted mother was viewed as the most important job one could have. Society understood the famous quote, "The hand that rocks the cradle is the hand that rules the world," and, thus, promoted parenthood. Not so today. Many women feel worthless without a career. It is a misconception that a stay-at-home parent has a minimal job. This is a lie; it's the most important job one could have. My mother postponed her profession until we were raised, and for that we are deeply grateful. While at home with her husband and three children, she was active in the community and helped my father with our family business, but she felt her greatest priority was in assuring the well-being of her family. My father made time in the evenings and weekends to help with sports and other activities; however, it was not until much later that he became a Christian.

What do you bring into a relationship? How is your relationship with Christ? A word to singles: many focus on finding the "right" person without first focusing on becoming the "right" person. **Why do so many marriages fail? In many cases, it's because they have religion and not a true relationship with Jesus.** In His words, "These people draw near to Me with their mouth, and honor Me with their lips, but their heart is far from Me" (Matthew 15:8). A.W. Tozer states, "Millions of professed believers talk as if [Christ] were real and act as if He were not. And always our actual position is to be discovered by the way we act, not by the way we talk." Again, it all starts here. The hammer of God must crush self-reliance. We must be *Desperate for More of Christ.*

How can we undo the emotional pain that we experience from failed relationships? We'll discuss this in more detail in the next chapter, but Jeremiah 29:13 has been a great comfort to me, "You will seek Me and find Me when you search for Me with all your heart." Don't allow past brokenness to cause future pain. Regret and failure will linger as long as we let them. Scripture is very clear: We are to forget those things that are behind us and focus on those things ahead. You can't change where you've been, but you can change where you're going.

# Discerning God's Will in Marriage

I've received many correspondences over the years, but this one is hard to forget. A young mother, thinking that she was in the center of God's will, sent my wife the following response after we encouraged her to continue in her marriage, "My decision is final. I'm leaving my husband. I know what the Bible says, but God knows my heart and wants me to be happy." How was this young mother so deceived? In short, she knew the Word, but did not obey it. She was living in deception (cf. James 1:22). Much had to do with the fact that she stopped attending church, no longer read her Bible, and began associating with people who drew her away from God. She lost sight of His will. The power of God's Word is in the application, not in the knowledge of it. Knowledge without obedience opens the door to deception.

Whether married for years or just a few days, most marriages fail because couples have difficulty discerning God's will, not only for their marriage, but for life in general. **I've found that a better understanding of God's will often leads to a better marriage.** There are far greater books written on knowing the will of God than what I can express in a few short pages, but I do want to outline certain principles that provide guidance for the journey.

Whether single or married, knowing the will of God is a desire we all should have, but unfortunately, many focus on the external circumstances of life and not on the inner condition of the heart. We may live in a certain location, have the job we want, and be married to the person of our choice, but often, many of our plans don't produce the peace or the fulfillment that we had hoped for, largely because we don't align our will with God's. We want what we think will make us happy—God wants to develop our character and marriage is often the tool He uses.

Although topics such as marriage and career are important to address, they don't supersede our need to address character development which often leads to joy. For instance, God's will for my life is centered less on what I do and more on who I am as a person. 2 Peter 1:5 reminds us that a life of moral excellence leads to knowing God better. One of the best ways to know God's plans are to live life according to His blueprints. This helps us respond better to our spouse and to difficult situations. I'm not promoting perfection, nor am I saying that God only guides a few obedient souls, but God does encourage obedience throughout the Scriptures. Determining God's will for our lives should be centered on developing a godly marriage rather than reaching a certain destination. Many times, the struggles that we encounter during marriage aren't necessarily an indicator that we are out of God's will (although at times they are), but rather, that He is molding us into His image. Instead of just asking, "What is God's will for my life?" we should also ask, "How can I develop and strengthen my marriage while pursuing His will?"

It's been said that in marriage you can tell cowards from heroes by watching which way they run when life because challenging—toward divorce court or toward God? It takes years to develop godly character and strengthen your marriage. **Don't get discouraged;**

**character is forged through affliction and tempered by adversity.** Character is built from the struggles we face and the obstacles we overcome.

Godly character can rebuild marriages, restore relationships, and influence others to follow our lead. In contrast, bad character can ruin marriage, destroy relationships, and draw the wrong crowd; therefore, the first step in seeking God's will for your marriage is to commit to developing godly character and then allow Him to direct your steps—"The steps of a good man are ordered by the Lord" (Psalms 37:23).

Since I recommitted my life to Christ, one of my personal goals has been to continually focus on character development, but I had no idea what I was asking. Imagine a young man entering the Marine Corps. He knows he wants to be a Marine but has no idea what to expect. The first day he is awe-struck by what's required of him, but the countless hours of training, the ongoing testing, and the discipline to remain committed eventually pay off and he graduates a Marine. Was the process easy? Hardly, it was the most difficult training he'd ever faced. One doesn't merely attend boot camp for a day, take a test and go home; the process is rigorous and intense. Likewise, when God molds and develops character, He does so to meet the challenges ahead and to prepare us for life. We too are tested, trained, and disciplined, but the rewards far outweigh the struggles. And this, too, is a process.

As a word of encouragement, the challenges we face such as difficult relationships, divorce, financial hardship, loss, illness, and so on, although extremely difficult, can draw us closer to God. How do we develop patience if we're not tested? How do we develop forgiveness if we are never wronged? How do we learn to trust God if we're never in need? James 1:2-4 states, "My brethren, count it all joy when you fall into various trials, knowing that the testing of your faith produces patience. But let patience have its perfect work, that you may be perfect and complete, lacking nothing." Focus on character more than comfort and you'll be happy with the outcome. Many times we have it in reverse order, we want to hear from God; then we'll work on our character. God says work on your character and then you'll be better able to hear Me.

I reiterate ... I'm not discounting the deep emotional pain of loss, illness, divorce, abuse, and so on; this type of pain is devastating and debilitating, but I do want to remind you that God makes provision for our pain and loss if we seek Him passionately, consistently, and unconditionally.

## Keys to Hearing God Clearly

When it comes to knowing God's will, more often than not, unless it's written in His Word, specific answers are often difficult to come by. For instance, the Bible doesn't say who to marry or where to work, but it does offer important principles that lead you in the right direction. However, there are some things that are clearly God's will for our lives: *to be saved and to worship Him, to be holy and set apart for His glory, to be filled continually with the Holy Spirit, to witness to others, to make disciples,* and so on. (Refer to 1

Timothy 2:4; 1 Thessalonians 4:3-7; Ephesians 5:17-18; and Matthew 28:19.)

Again, although the following pages will not outline God's specific will for your life, they will provide guidance for the journey.

- *Recognize that God's will is not as clearly defined as a road map.* How often do we pray, "Should I get married?" Some even pray, "Should I divorce my spouse?" The "should I's" can be endless. God's will is a journey as well as a destination. God told Abraham in Genesis 12:1 to go to a land that He would show him, and so it is with us. He teaches us to sense His direction through His Word and the guidance of the Holy Spirit. Sometimes we do experience a true sense of God's exact direction, but often, we simply walk by faith. Don't look back and regret your marriage, even if it seems unclear and hazy at times. Generally, it's simply a matter of the Proverbs 3:6 acknowledgement: pray, commit your ways to Him daily, and move in a forward direction trusting that He is directing your path. His will and His Word always align.

- *Compare what you're feeling to the Word of God.* How often do we sense a stirring in our spirit and are not sure if it's God or not? Sadly, many who divorce or separate make comments such as, "God just wants me to be happy," or "I feel that God is leading me." Be very careful here. God's will always corresponds with His Word. For example, many Christians date and marry nonbelievers. Regardless of feelings, God's

Word is clear on this point. Does this mean that God cannot bless a Christian if he or she marries an unbeliever? No, but being equally yoked is not just a good idea; it's a principle that promotes a healthy and strong marriage. I'm not suggesting that spouses turn a deaf ear to substance abuse, violence, dishonesty, lying, cheating, and severe problems with lust; God may have them step away from the situation for a season, but I also believe that God can redeem our marriage when we truly look to Him. The motive behind such a move should be restoration rather than divorce. The more we ignore God's leading, the harder it becomes to hear His voice; hence, we become spiritually deaf. Again, check the leading against Scripture. Does it line up? If you sense that you are going in a wrong direction, or are not sure, step away and take time to wait and pray. You can't go wrong by being patient as you seek God's will.

- *Patiently and quietly listen.* When I first met my wife, we prayed and waited patiently. Our desire to marry continued to grow and many godly people confirmed the decision. Many of us lead very busy lives which makes it difficult to be in the right frame of mind to hear from God. It wasn't until we continued to spend each morning in solitude and prayer that we began to sense God's direction. We had peace as the date approached. From my experience, I found that God doesn't always say yes or no immediately; He tells us to wait and be patient. His leading isn't a thoughtless course of action; it's a well designed plan that requires patience. Patience builds godly character, character builds fortitude, and fortitude leads to perseverance. On another note, it's incredibly difficult to hear God if we're actively engaging in sin. Sin means to miss the mark—we can't be on target in the center of God's will if we're always missing the mark. My counsel to those considering divorce rarely changes: pray, wait, and obey. Pray to God often and set aside time to worship and study His Word, wait for direction, and obey His principles. Then start the process over again. In some cases, separation (with the hope of reconciliation) can aid in this process. Time alone sometimes helps the situation; it can be a wake-up call. When spouses are looking forward to divorce in order to find someone new, it's likely that they are not patiently and quietly waiting on God, and it may well mean a repeat of the same a few years later.

- *Keep moving.* You might ask, "If we are to patiently wait and quietly listen, how can we keep moving?" Although there are clearly times when God wants us to stand still, it's hard to give direction to what's not moving. During my childhood and teen years, my family often vacationed and fished in the Eastern Sierra Nevada Mountain Range in California. Once on the lake, dad would accelerate the boat motor and head off until we reached our fishing destination. He'd shut off the motor and lower the anchor. On one occasion when I was very young, I tried steering the boat. No matter what direction I turned the wheel, the boat stood still. I asked my dad why the boat wasn't working. He said that it was working but that it could not be steered unless it was moving. In the same way, God may be directing us, but if we're not moving we won't get anywhere. Moving doesn't mean walking around without an agenda—it means serving God and others. When God heals a marriage, it's often when we're moving in the right direction, not looking in the wrong direction. Did you catch that? When God heals a marriage, it's often when we're moving in the right direction, not looking in the wrong direction.

- *His will is often revealed over time.* Most of us want immediate answers, but more often than not, God's will tends to be a process rather than an instant revelation. Granted, there are times when the Holy Spirit directs us instantly—prompting a phone call to a friend in need, or leading us to make a quick decision, but we usually see only snap-shots of the big picture. God wants us to walk in faith and trust in Him. From my pastoral experience, I estimate that most divorces are rushed. Instead of desperately seeking God for direction, most spouses desire a new relationship. I vividly remember talking to a woman who was divorcing her husband. Her comment during the divorce caught me off guard, "Pastor, I'm ready to marry again and get on with my life." I lovingly challenged her on the condition of her heart, but she was not open for feedback ... she was ready to move on. Not surprisingly, she struggled with depression and anxiety; she had no peace. In my opinion, she was out of God's will because she was in a hurry. 1 Corinthians 7:10-11 immediately came to mind, "A wife must not leave her husband. But if she does leave him, let her remain single or else go back to him. And the husband must not leave the wife." This clearly states that she should remain single or be reconciled. Because of their profoundly different backgrounds—my mother was from Southern California and my father was from Oklahoma—my parent's marriage was often a challenge, but they were committed to one another and their relationship grew as a result.

- *Don't be surprised by challenges.* For years, I believed that marriage was easy while in the center of God's will, and that if marriage wasn't easy we were out of His will. This is not necessarily true. Yes, we should have peace in the center of God's will, but, at times, we may fight bouts of anxiety, depression, difficulties, and fear. Many Biblical heroes fought hardship and anxiety while being in the center of God's will. Abraham, Sarah, Moses, Joseph, Elijah, Jeremiah, Isaiah, Ruth, Mary, the Apostle Paul, the Disciples, etc., all faced difficult times and challenging circumstances. I can't think of anyone of significance in the Bible who wasn't challenged by adversity. Our first year of marriage was very difficult, and after our first child was born another season of difficulty arose. Was this an indicator that we were out of God's will? Of course not. Even though we "felt" (there goes those "feelings" again) that we were outside of His will, we soon realized that pride and selfishness were the main culprits, and a lack of sleep with a newborn at home. We repented, apologized, and recognized our immature attitudes. We agreed to trust God and keep moving forward. Was it easy? Hardly. However, within a few weeks we saw a noticeable difference. How did we regain traction? First, we focused on God's moral will for our lives (i.e., purity, honesty, love, humility, etc.). Second, we focused on obeying His principle to love regardless of "feelings." Third, we used wisdom, and relied on Him to guide us. Was it trouble-free? Not at all, my first marriage had ended in divorce. Although I was scripturally released, it had made me fearful of starting over again. Morgan's issues with self-esteem continued to contribute to her anxiety— this type of thing is the "personal baggage" you often hear referred to. Extra baggage does not make the journey wrong; it simply means there's more to carry. Unquestionably, being in the center of God's will does not prevent challenges, it often creates them. But as long as we were following His direction and obeying His principles, we felt confident that He would direct our path.

- *God's will is always what's best for you.* I remember feeling, as a teen, that when I committed my life to Christ all the fun would be over and He might send me to a mission field. You probably know people who feel this way—maybe that's you. Nothing could be farther from the truth; God's will is always what's best for you although it may not feel like it from time to time. He places godly desires within all of us, and those desires will manifest themselves as we pursue His will. I've listened to dozens of missionaries speak and all of them felt the calling and had a deep desire to serve God in that arena. I've also talked to many Christian businessmen and professionals, and they too felt inclined toward their specific field. God does not give talent and interests to be wasted; He encourages the desires of your heart as you seek to serve Him and others—God is the one who places the desire within you. *Many marriages fail because we have ulterior motives ... we expected to get rather than to give.* An important step to knowing God's will in your marriage is to realize that His will is always better than ours.

- *His leading is calm and reassuring.* God rarely rushes. If you feel rushed to divorce, which often leads to confusion, wait on God and ask for clarity. Although there may be times when we must make a quick, timely decision, if you feel rushed, simply stop and wait. If, for some reason, you can't wait, simply use wisdom and make the decision to the best of your ability. Slow down, position yourself in His will, and wait on Him. You can rarely go wrong waiting, but you can often go wrong rushing.

## Our First Priority—It May Surprise You

Once I married my wife, I recognized the need to truly love her, but not the way the world sees love—the way God designed it. To do this, I needed to work on patience, kindness, and servitude, and to begin to trust, believe, and to protect. This didn't mean that I was to avoid red flags when we dated, but there's a difference between red flags and workable issues.

As a side note to those not yet married: when unsure if areas of concern are red flag's or simply issues to work through, it's helpful to first ask ... can we work through these problems together and with counsel, or do they need to be dealt with individually before marriage? Second, are these issues going to cause severe problems in the future? For example, if Morgan's jealously created a severe lack of trust, thus, putting a tremendous strain on the relationship, it may have been wise to put the relationship on hold. In the same way, if my tendency towards selfishness caused her neglect, it would have been wise for her to reconsider the relationship, but since our issues were not severe, we committed to work on them together. Much of it depends on the individual and the circumstances. If you notice obvious red flags while dating such as discussed earlier—substance abuse, violence, dishonesty, lying, cheating, or problems with lust and anger, then in most cases, it's time to question the relationship ... at least for now.

Now back on course ... how should we love? No, this isn't a trick question. If love is the greatest commandment then it needs to be our first priority. When our view of love is distorted, we get into trouble. For example, attraction is not love, its attraction—a pull toward a particular person or thing. Countless couples say that they are in love when, in reality, they are attracted. Attraction comes and goes, but "true" love remains forever. Most would agree, however, that attraction is initially what draws us together. Ideally, attraction continues throughout marriage, however, the spiritual essence of love gives it holding power.

The Bible defines love, "Love is patient, love is kind. It does not envy, it does not boast, it is not proud. It is not rude, it is not self-seeking, it is not easily angered, it keeps no record of wrongs. Love does not delight in evil but rejoices with the truth. It always protects, always trusts, always hopes, always perseveres" (1 Corinthians 13:4-7 NIV). This is how we are to love... our spouses, our friends, our children, etc.

*Love is patient and kind ...*

We should be patient and understanding with the needs of others. Patience and kindness actually run side-by-side. Kindness means to show a tender, considerate, and helping nature toward another... to be patient. This could simply mean being patient and kind as your partner takes twice as long as you to get ready, or it may require more patience and kindness (grace) as they work through their weaknesses. Patience means taking time to be supportive and understanding, and not allowing our needs to get in the way of their needs. There are times, however, when you will need to talk to your spouse when their requests or expectations seem unreasonable. Begin by asking that God change them and that He show you where you may need to change as well. Reserve a night to relax and share, in a non-threatening manner, what's on your mind; both should share, with no interruptions. It should be a time to truly listen and to try to understand the needs of the other person. Affirm their feelings even though you may not agree with them. There is wise counsel in the words, seek first to understand and then to be understood. Repeat back what is said to make sure that what is said is what is heard.

We're often misunderstood and we sometimes fail to meet the need of another for a practical reason rather than a selfish motive. Patience also means not rushing the relationship..."true love waits." Unfortunately, many couples rush the courting process because of their desire for physical intimacy. They may feel that if God brought them together, He must want them to marry soon; only to later find that marriage was not the right choice.

*Love does not envy or boast, nor is it proud ...*

When envy enters our heart, it's difficult to love the way God intended. Envy or jealousy in a relationship can occur when couples view their relationship as competition rather than commitment to cooperate. This may happen when two people are actively involved together in ministry, school, or careers. If not careful, they may compete with one another rather than pursue their dreams together. It's important to encourage the success of one another as well as the relationship.

*Keep no record of wrong, nor delight in evil ...*

It has been said that relationships are like checking accounts. Words of healing and praise are deposits into our emotional bank account; whereas words of anger and insults are withdrawals. If there are more withdrawals than deposits, the account not only loses value but it can create emotional bankruptcy. Emotional bankruptcy happens frequently in relationships, especially marriage. Learn to make deposits and avoid withdrawals if you want a lasting, meaningful relationship. From time to time, we say and do things that hurt others; others say and do things that hurt us. God instructs us to overlook the wrongs done against us, and hopefully others will do the same and keep the account open. (I'm not referring to allowing chronic physical, emotional, or verbal abuse. If you are dating and this is a problem, stop! If you are married, seek help from those who will give scriptural counsel and never underestimate the power of prayer.)

Sometimes we attack one another, and although done in humor, words carry enormous weight. If a husband or wife is continually called lazy or bothersome, his or her self-esteem will eventually deteriorate and the relationship will lose its value. One very common, indirect insult is to ask your spouse what he or she has done all day. The Bible directs us to "be slow to speak" (James 1:19). God wants us to think before we speak and/or react.

*Love always hopes, trusts, protects and perseveres ...*

Hope means to anticipate, expect, or to look forward to something. Love hopes for and believes the best in others. It is translated through our actions and our words. We may not always see the best in others, but we trust that it is there and we encourage it to grow.

Love that protects, defends and guards the integrity of others is the kind of love that we want to develop with our spouse. It may also be demonstrated through acts of heroism that we frequently see. When dating or courting, protect the feelings and emotions of others by guarding their hearts as well as yours.

Finally, perseverance is the principle that holds us together. It is the "stick-to-it-iveness" that binds us together during hard times when we're tempted to walk away. As mentioned earlier, studies indicate that couples who report being unhappy, when interviewed a few years later, reported being happy, and very happy that they remained together.

Let me take the opportunity, at this point, to address the harm in living together before marriage. The cultural concept of living together does not allow for perseverance. In essence, it states that there is no need to work through challenges because there is no solid commitment. Without a commitment to "work-through," individuals move from relationship to relationship and never develop a strong union—working through challenges is the very ingredient that builds lasting relationships. Couples today want the freedom to divorce and leave the marriage if it doesn't work out. Marriage never works out, you have to work it out. In addition to being out of God's will, living together fails to offer this most important factor, and thus, defeats itself.

My father was known in our valley for his ability to understand the lay of the land, the condition of the soil, and water tables. Land owners would sometimes consult him before building. Several small communities nestled in the foothills near our home were developed around small lakes, and thus, very high water tables and unstable ground. My father would sometimes comment about his concern for residents who chose to buy or build a home on questionable ground because of view and location. In time, several families were forced to relocate due to rising water levels. The cost to repair or maintain homes would sometimes cost tens of thousands of dollars.

A stable foundation is also essential in developing a healthy marriage. For example, a wife may find that after a year of marriage her husband has a "wandering eye" and is involved in sexual sin. The root of the problem isn't necessarily his wandering eye (although that is a problem). The real problem was the foundation on which his life was built. Did she choose a person of character? Did he demonstrate integrity? Did he have positive role models in his life? Did he seek God wholeheartedly? These are questions to ask before marriage. **Unfortunately, many overlook a weak foundation because they like the view.** Singles often overlook major character flaws because they like how the person looks or makes them feel. It's primarily the foundation (character) not the view (external looks) that determines success or failure in a marriage, especially through adversity. The inner qualities of a gracious heart are enduring but outer beauty is fleeting. Ask yourself, "If you take away the body, what do you have?" In time, that body will change and hopefully you'll be happy with the person inside.

Marriage is like a race of endurance, full of wonderful opportunities and experiences. There are also occasional roadblocks, delays, pitfalls, and hurdles. Make no mistake about it—we win by persevering, by getting up and not giving in. Successful marriages are often built from failure. Actually, successful people often fail more than failures do; people who have failed simply refuse to give up.

A word about forgiveness here. Few things hurt us more than failing to forgive others or ourselves from past mistakes. Many times memories haunt and discourage us from moving forward. As a result, people often rate themselves according to what they were, or what they did, not realizing that who they are now, and who they will become is far more important.

## It Begins Inwardly and Spreads Out

The power to persevere is one of the greatest attributes that we possess. Learning from experience empowers us to move forward. There is little we can do about life's glitches except control the way we respond to them. Remember, the obstacles ahead are not greater than God's power to take you through.

Society tends to program our looks and actions. Women, as well as young girls, reference magazines to see how they should dress and act; teenage boys consult TV and the media for role models, and many men today measure their self worth by what they have accomplished in business and financially, not realizing that relationship with God, family, and others is the treasure they should be seeking. It's little wonder that the family structure is rapidly disintegrating. It begins inwardly and spreads out.

The true message of this chapter is simple and straightforward: Christ is our only hope ... your only hope. Additionally, character qualities such as discipline, perseverance, patience, and commitment are eroding from today's society. As a result, marriages, families, and relationships are falling apart. Failure to adhere to these basic principles has eroded our lives, like water and time has eroded the banks of the Colorado River and formed the Grand Canyon. We are often unaware until the work is done. Erosion has the power to change a mighty rivers course; surely it can change the course of our lives as well. Don't allow a declining cultural mind-set to erode essential qualities in your life. Build on the solid rock of God's Word. It's never too late to be *Desperate for More of Him.*

## EBook Sermon Links:

Early in 2012, I used the *Real Marriage* promotional material (and a few sermon titles) from Mars Hill, Seattle with their permission, but I provided my own sermon content. The eight messages from the sermon series are below:

1. Wilt Thou not Revive us Again:
   https://vimeo.com/36362334

2. Breaking up Fallow Ground:
   https://vimeo.com/36792777

3. Removing Destructive Influences:
   https://vimeo.com/37306907

4. Understanding & Appreciating Roles [part 1]:
   https://vimeo.com/37573839

5. Understanding & Appreciating Roles [part 2]:
   https://vimeo.com/38034291

6. Anger—The Great Destroyer:
   https://vimeo.com/38465301

7. SEX—Gross, Good, or god?:
   https://vimeo.com/38945947

8. Divorce—Hope for the Hurting:
   https://vimeo.com/39250214

# CHAPTER SIX: Group Study Questions

1. In regard to Scripture, if we apply only the ones we want to our marriage, how can we easily miss what we need? List at least two examples of picking and choosing Scriptures. (For example, Ephesians 5:22 is often used in abusive relationships to control and to manipulate.)

2. Do you agree that marriage can be a wonderful sanctification tool if we allow the hammer of God to shape us? List ways that marriage builds and shapes character.

3. How important is obedience when it comes to discerning the will of God? Take time and read James 1:22 before commenting.

4. Many believe that marriage is easy while in the center of God's will, and that if marriage isn't easy then we are out of His will. How can this faulty thinking obstruct a healthy view of marriage?

5. Marriage is like a race of endurance, full of wonderful opportunities and experiences. There are also occasional roadblocks, delays, pitfalls, and hurdles. How can we overcome them?

# CHAPTER SEVEN: *Desperate for Emotional Healing*

# Divorce—Hope for the Hurting

"The emotional pain and brokenness that I experienced from divorce was greater than the pain of the concentration camps."

*Holocaust Survivor*

A few years ago, I was listening to a syndicated Christian radio program. A survivor of the holocaust was being interviewed. She described the horrific conditions of the concentration camps and then made a statement I'd never forget. She described the emotional pain and the brokenness she experienced from her divorce as greater than the pain of the concentration camp. Six months later, another guest on the same program, described the pain of losing her husband to cancer. She spoke about how his illness devastated their lives after ten long months of suffering. I was again moved to hear her say that she would have rather lost her husband to death by cancer than divorce.

Unbelievable! Two women, with entirely different stories, who had gone through more pain than many of us will ever know said that divorce is, or would be, more painful than death. Why was divorce more devastating than a concentration camp or cancer? Death is a natural process and God makes provision, but the spiritual union of two people was never designed to be broken aside from death— we are vulnerable in divorce and the pain is lasting. We may try to hide the pain that lingers, but it's always there waiting for the opportunity to rise again. Unless God rebuilds the foundation, those divorced may find themselves in the same situation with the second, third, or fourth spouse.

The good news, however, is that both of the women referenced God's healing power. Regardless of what they had endured, God delivered them from emotional scares and feelings of abandonment. Since divorce affects nearly half the population, we must ask God to deliver families from the pain and break the walls that imprison. Emotional healing is vital when seeking the heart of God. Past pain, resentment, bitterness, anger, and un-forgiveness can prevent us from being *Desperate for More of God*.

In the book, *Sacred Thirst*, the author writes,

"The bride and groom are standing in front of everyone, looking better than they are ever going to look again, getting so much attention and affirmation. Everybody even stands when they walk in so it's easy to think this marriage, at least, is about them. It's not. Just look at the worn-out parents sitting in the first pew—they understand this. The only reason these parents are still married is because long ago they learned how to handle the hurt they caused each other. They know that the last thing you ever want to do with hurt is to let it define you."[20]

This last statement offers one of the most profound points that I've read on brokenness. Those who do not allow hurt to entrap them can turn brokenness into a dynamic relationship with God, but those shackled by past pain are truly imprisoned by it. **Married or divorced, the walls we build to protect may eventually imprison.**

How can we undo the emotional pain that we experience from failed relationships? First, we must understand that it's not an external fight, it's an internal struggle: "For we do not wrestle against flesh and blood, but against principalities, against powers, against the rulers of the darkness of this age, against spiritual hosts of wickedness in the heavenly places" (Ephesians 6:12). God works within us by transmitting healthy thoughts into godly actions. Our mind is where battles are either won or lost. Those who do not forgive or release bitterness, anger, and hurt, never experience freedom, happiness, or "true" restoration. It all starts here.

Ephesians 4:31-32 says to "let all bitterness, wrath, anger, clamor, and evil speaking be put away from you, with all malice. And be kind to one another, tenderhearted, forgiving one another, even as God in Christ forgave you." Simply stated, whether you were a victim of a failed marriage, or the offender, if you fail to forgive, bitterness and anger, though skillfully masked, can and will hinder your relationship with God and others. Married, divorced, separated, or single, God can turn brokenness into an unbreakable force, but it is imperative that your mind is renewed by applying biblical principles, beginning with forgiveness.

Those who have walked in true forgiveness know that God restores. **It's been well stated that life makes us bitter or it makes us better—the choice is ours.** Secondly, destructive strongholds, influences, and addictions must be dealt with. God can deliver those broken by a failed marriage, but in order for change to occur on the outside (i.e., remarriage or restoration) it first must occur on the inside. Strongholds include bitterness, pride, lust, selfishness, substance abuse, toxic relationships, anger, and physical abuse, to name a few. These destructive influences hinder the healing and rebuilding process, as well as a deeper walk with God. Healing begins with a commitment to work on those areas known to be detrimental to your spiritual health and the health of the relationship.

Our attitude should be one in which we surrender our entire lifestyle to God. I've spoken with many who admitted that alcohol or substance abuse ruined their relationship, but instead of surrendering the problem to God and breaking the addiction, they simply found someone else to tolerate their habit. Unfortunately, in most cases, the problem surfaced again.

It's little wonder that many go through life changing partners, careers, or residency searching for someone or something that can never be found apart from the wholeness that a personal relationship with Christ brings. If this is you, I encourage you to stop wandering from relationship to relationship and allow God to rebuild and restore: "Therefore repent and return, so that your sins may be wiped away, in order that times of refreshing may come from the presence of the Lord" (Acts 3:19).

Do you desire peace and joy again? Simply return to God: "You will seek Me and find Me when you search for Me with all your heart" (Jeremiah 29:13). Full surrender provides fertile ground for joy and peace. If you're like me, you may realize that many years of "wandering" could have been avoided. Many, no doubt, had clear direction for their marriage, but because of selfishness, disobedience, disregard, or a deaf ear to God's direction, it ended in divorce ... but God can rebuild and redeem your life. Don't allow past brokenness to cause future pain. Regret and failure will linger as long as we let them. **You can't change where you've been, but you can change where you're going.**

Recall the earlier mention of shepherds who would break the leg of a lamb that continually wandered from the flock and, thus, the shepherd's protection. The shepherd would then splint the broken leg and carry the lamb on his shoulders for weeks until the leg healed. As painful as this was for the lamb, it was necessary to protect it from being ravished by wolves or other predators. In time, through the broken and dependent relationship, the lamb learned to walk and to remain in the protective presence of his shepherd. This concept was well stated by David in Psalms 51:8, "That the bones You have broken may rejoice." And Isaiah reminds us, "All we like sheep have gone astray" (53:6). Ironically, many thank the Lord for using their divorce to bring them back to the Good Shepherd. They better understand Paul's words in Philippians 3:10, "that I may know Him and the power of His resurrection, and the fellowship of His sufferings...". Power and suffering go hand-in-hand. How do you know God as Provider if you are never in need? How do you know Him as Healer if you are never sick? How do you know Him as Restorer if you are never broken? **The power of the Christian life is only found in God's power to sustain.**

What will it take to bring you back to the Good Shepherd? A deliberate decision to stay close to the Him can avoid unneeded pain and provide safety and protection; it's the first step in the rebuilding process.

## Divorce—Seeking to Clear the Confusion

Perhaps one of the most difficult Scriptures dealing with divorce or separation is 1 Corinthians 7:10-11, "Now to the married I command, yet not I but the Lord: A wife is not to depart from her husband. But even if she does depart, let her remain unmarried or be reconciled to her husband. And a husband is not to divorce his wife." This clearly states that those who are divorced and/or separated, unless "scripturally released," should not remarry, but instead, seek restoration or stay single. This Scripture should create more serious consideration before marriage, and be a deterrent to divorce. Lack of regard for this Scripture has taken us to the other extreme—no fault divorce.

1 Corinthians 7:15 adds that if the spouse who isn't a Christian insists on leaving, that we are to let them go. God wants His children to live in peace. This Scripture has been repeatedly misused for personal advantage. Even though actions of a spouse may resemble that of an unbeliever because they choose to leave, hard questions

need to be asked. For example, if extreme anger, verbal or physical abuse, or frantic controlling and manipulating are occurring, a spouse may leave for a season with the goal and hope of restoration. *In this case, the spouse leaves because the environment is unbearable, not because they are an unbeliever.*

What if an unbelieving spouse walks away and has no desire of returning? Depending on the circumstances, 1 Corinthians 7:15 seems to indicate that the other is released, but it's wise to not rush ahead into something new. Some spouses never return while others leave for a season—blatant disrespect, financial irresponsibility, pornography, and so on, can also drive a spouse away.

Clearly understand that I'm not advocating separation, divorce, or remaining in an abusive relationship, nor am I saying that if you are currently separated, that divorce become an option because better opportunities await you. **God hates divorce and anyone who has been there knows why.** This chapter is not designed to be a one-size-fits-all approach ... there are too many variables to address every situation. The purpose of this chapter is to offer hope, wisdom, and insight from a biblical perspective.

I believe, first and foremost, in reconciliation and restoration but these are not always options. That's why a personal relationship with Jesus and obedience to His Word is profoundly important, especially when you don't "feel" like it. Through that relationship you will be able to make the right decision. It won't be easy because lives have been damaged, dreams destroyed, and promises broken, but God continually draws us back through His forgiveness. God desires that we know His will and follow His lead in spite of detours.

Even when 1 Corinthians 7:15 applies, it's wise to allow a significant amount of time to pass before moving forward. This may reveal if the person left only for a season, or has chosen to leave permanently. For instance, before I began seriously dating my wife, I contacted my ex-wife nearly three years after our divorce to validate my feelings of being released from our past relationship and to see if there was any hope of restoration. She confirmed that she was in a long-term relationship that would eventually lead to marriage, and she wished me the best. I felt that I had received my last and most solid confirmation to move forward.

One of the biggest mistakes when considering restoration or seeking direction is to become involved in another relationship soon after the divorce or separation. God could be working in the life of the other spouse even though His work can't be seen. They may even become hostile and angry. Things often get worse before they get better. Jumping into a new relationship severely hinders any chance of reconciliation, as well as the ability to follow God's lead.

I'm astonished at the number of people with back-up plans. They keep a boyfriend or girlfriend on the back-burner just in case restoration does not occur. This thought process is far removed from God's will. Do we honestly think that God is pleased with back-up plans? Restoration does not always happen quickly... what takes years to destroy may take years to rebuild. Patience is the key. A person who is truly *Desperate for More of God* will wait on Him. They will not rush into a new relationship. Sadly, many twist the Scriptures so they can pursue other relationships.

Seeking advice or counsel during a separation requires good judgment. It may be tempting to accept the advice of others even though not scripturally sound. Counseling with those skilled in the Word is invaluable, and desperately needed, but all the counseling in the world will not work if the heart is not right. God heals us primarily with the transforming power of His Word and repentance through a broken heart: "He sent His word and healed them, and delivered them from their destructions" (Psalm 107:20). Deep heart-felt repentance leads to "times of refreshing from the presence of the Lord" (cf. Acts 3:19).

One goal of counseling is to take people back to the Word. Spouses must spend extended time in the Word with an open and teachable heart. My intent is not to disregard counseling—I do it daily and seek it often—I also don't want to disregard the emotional pain of brokenness; I've experienced it myself. But I do want to remind you that God restores us primarily through obedience to His Word, along with faith, patience, and forgiveness.

We live in deception and futility when we fight against the spiritual principle of obedience. We only delude ourselves when we look for those who tell us what we want to hear, not what we need to hear. God's Word often does the opposite... it reveals the heart and does not validate sin. The Word does not coddle feelings like some tend to do; it crushes them so that repentance takes place. It also builds and restores.

When we justify sinful behavior, genuine repentance has not taken place. We become very good with our words; very good at excusing actions. Blame deflects responsibility—it excuses actions and prevents genuine repentance from taking place. Don't twist the Scriptures or make excuses. Surrender the entire relationship to God and trust Him to see you through.

Again, marriage today is not failing because it's more difficult than in years past—it's failing because the foundation has weakened. A "genuine" relationship with Christ is the solid rock upon which marriage must be built. Sadly, most are neglecting this foundational truth. Do you have a genuine relationship with Christ, or are you simply going through the motions? It all begins here.

## Divorce and Separation—is Restoration Always God's Will?

In my opinion, only God can truly answer this question. We must seek Him wholeheartedly and unconditionally for direction. Spouses are encouraged to spend extended time in the Word and obedience to it, as well as extended times of prayer and fasting, and seeking godly counsel. All destructive relationships and toxic counsel must be severed as you seek to answer this question.

From time to time, it may be wise to temporarily stop seeking counsel. Instead, spend more time seeking God. A counselor can only offer input from his or her perspective, albeit from a biblical perspective, but God often cuts right to the heart of the matter and brings peace where there is confusion, rest where there is anxiety, and joy where there is sorrow. Too many of us seek the opinions of others and neglect the One who has the answers.

Many great Bible teachers are divided on this issue of divorce. Some believe that re-marriage to another is never allowed unless one of the spouses dies, but others suggest that it is permissible when adultery and abandonment occur. One thing is certain, if the Scriptures on marriage and divorce were fully taught and obeyed they would create more serious consideration before marriage, and would be a great deterrent to divorce. Again, lack of regard for the Scriptures has taken us to the other extreme—no fault divorce.

God hates divorce; reconciliation is pleasing to Him. He is the God of reconciliation. There are instances, in my opinion, when one is released through consistent unfaithfulness and/or abandonment; however, reconciliation should still be sought. First and foremost, God's will is that we walk in integrity, follow His principles, use wisdom, be patient, and seek Him during the journey. For some, reconciliation may result, for others it may not.

When reconciliation does not occur, the enemy often resurrects past failures to hinder peace and joy. For instance, as my wife Morgan and I began our relationship a few years after my divorce, I would become excited about our future, but I also became very fearful. I did not want to experience the pain of divorce again. I was like a man who fell off a horse and was afraid to ride again, but as we moved forward in the relationship, anxiety and confusion gave way to peace, joy, and fulfillment as we both sought God wholeheartedly.

If you are separated, or recently divorced, and are lacking peace and joy, I encourage you to re-think your current situation. Granted, it's difficult to be consistently joyful when separated or recently divorced, but confusion, anxiety, fear, and depression are sometimes indicators that we are outside of God's will. (Please note the word "sometimes.") Don't trust feelings over Scripture by saying, "I know what the Bible says, but God wants me to be happy. He knows my heart." How can I say "hog-wash" politely? This statement simply reveals the sinfulness and outright deception of the human heart. God is not a doting grandfather who simply looks the other way when His children sin.

**God has given us the freedom to choose, and, in marriage, the choices of one will affect the life of the other.** If your spouse has left, and you've waited and have done all that you can do biblically, I believe that God will look at your heart more than your circumstances. King David was not able to build the temple because of his past—he was a man of war, but God said, "Whereas it was in your heart to build a temple for My name, you did well in that it was in your heart" (2 Chronicles 6:8). Contextually, this verse is not dealing with marriage, but the overlapping principle applies: because David's heart was right, God continued to direct him.

Many often thank God for using their divorce to bring them back to Him. I don't believe that God necessarily causes divorce, but He can use it to bring the prodigal home. We also know that what the enemy intends for evil, God can use for good. Divorce is often the result of bad decisions, anger, and misguided focus, but, contrary to what some believe, it is not the unpardonable sin; rejecting Christ is. Many divorced Christians carry years of regret into future relationships. If God is doing a new thing, it's vitally important that past brokenness does not prevent future plans. But if God is ministering restoration in your spirit, wait for it; contend for it; pray fervently for it. I also encourage you to remove everything that can hinder restoration (e.g., wrong relationships, strongholds, addictions, anger, un-forgiveness, bitterness, etc.). I cannot emphasize this enough. Seek Him wholeheartedly and unconditionally. God, not a new relationship, is all that you need right now. He will direct you ... this I know.

## Feelings Can Lie—Obedience Can be Trusted

In the eyes of a secular culture, obedience to God's Word seems intolerant, tyrannical, and demanding. Yet, obedience is a spiritual principle intended to protect and honor others, as well as ourselves. Sadly, it is not only a cultural mindset, but many Christians have little regard for, or a skewed understanding of obedience.

One of the most common comments I've heard is, "I know what the Bible says! I've been in church all of my life, but...". People often hear, but "hearing" is not enough.

Jesus confirmed this in Luke 6:49 when He said that the person who hears His words but does not put them into practice is like a man who builds a house without a foundation. When the storm comes, it collapses. We must not only hear God's Word, we must respond. **A consistent theme throughout the Bible is: hearing plus doing equals success.**

We live in a nation saturated with hearing. The Bible is readily accessible in many translations. Greek and Hebrew resources are in abundance. Classes on homiletics and hermeneutics are flourishing. Hundreds of Christian radio stations and tens of thousands of sermon podcasts are aired daily. We are inundated with the Word of God. So what's the problem? Why so many broken lives and families? The problem is, and has always been, obedience. In Genesis 4:7, near the beginning of the creation of man, we read God's words to Cain, "If you do well, will you not be accepted? And if you do not do well, sin is crouching at the door. Its desire is for you, but you must rule over it." Obedience matters. For example, I remember counseling a man about his anger. His response was, "I know what the Bible says!" He then offered many excuses and justified his behavior. One of the frustrations of counseling is that many say the right thing, and often quote Scripture, but few genuinely repent and obey the Word. The power of the Word is in the obedience to it.

On numerous occasions when I speak about the dangerous of sexual sin, many enthusiastically agree that it's wrong, but continue anyway ("hear" but do not "do"). Again, sexual sin is deceptive ... it draws us in to a false sense of attraction. Lust is extremely strong and enticing.

It affects emotions, feelings, and our will at a very deep level. For those who are married, it often leads to the devastating words, "I don't love you anymore." At this point, unable to perceive and/or obey spiritual truth, sin's deception has taken over and spiritual blindness has set in.

When sin has gained a stronghold through lust, bitterness, anger, gossip, jealousy, lying, and so on, the heart hardens and an array of excuses follows. In the case of sexual sin, the spouse they once loved and cherished is now despised and discarded. Sin continues to deceive with the ultimate goal of killing the marriage: "Sin when it is fully grown brings forth death" (James 1:15).

Obedience is crucial; it stops sin dead in its tracks. The only way out of sins path is to do what is right regardless of feelings. Feelings can lie, but obedience can be trusted. Sadly, many do not experience freedom and true restoration because wholeness is found in obeying the truth, not just in hearing it. Church, for some, serves as therapy for this very reason. They hear about sin, are convicted, and leave feeling justified because they "heard" and "felt," but they did not repent and change. Genuine faith is reflected in obedience to God and His Word. The fruit that follows is sincere humility, selfless love, true repentance, and disengagement from the things of the world versus a love for them. Does your life reflect these characteristics? As you can see, hearing and obeying the truth are vitally important. Begin here ... you'll be amazed at the difference obedience makes.

# Divorce—When to Hold on ... When to Move on

In the chapter written primarily to men, I made the following observation in the next two paragraphs. The Bible describes the intoxicating power of passion associated with lust and adultery. Misdirected passion deceives, misleads, and influences ... we walk in darkness, stumbling ... unable to see what we stumble over. This description well explains why so many caught in sexual sin describe a sense of confusion and a disconnection from God. Adultery moves us from the altar to the courtroom—transforming a couple, once deeply in love, into bitter enemies. Hopes and dreams for the birth of a child, now twisted, become a nightmare for innocent children. Adultery is selfishness at its core. If you are currently dating someone while separated, or if he or she is separated, you are walking on very thin ice.

**How sad that sexual appetites often devour our own children, as well as ourselves.** Proverbs 9:17-18 describes adultery, "Stolen water is sweet, and bread eaten in secret is pleasant. But he does not know that the dead are there, that her guests are in the depths of hell." Adultery hardens the heart toward spouses ... those who were once loved and cherished now feel insignificant and discarded. Children often feel to blame for not being good enough ... trying hard enough. God help our selfish hearts! It would seem that for loving parents, the thought of this horror would bring sexual sin to a sobering halt.

The pain of adultery can make us bitter, or it can make us better—ultimately, it's our choice. God can restore if the person is willing to admit that he or she was wrong. True repentance is unconditional and takes full responsibility for wrongs done. A truly repent person is desperate to be forgiven rather than placing blame or responsibility on others. Don't misunderstand, both spouses have work to do, but this comes later.

I went on to discuss with the men the two areas that often prevent reconciliation. If you are a woman, feel free to read that section as well. There is hope. Don't give up; look up. There are consequences for past mistakes, but the answer is to live in God's arms redeemed rather than to live broken outside of His will. Which way will you run?

Back to the question, "When should a person hold on for restoration, or move on with his or her life?" Only God can truly answer this question, but patience, long-suffering, and forgiveness must be sought. If God is ministering restoration in your spirit, wait for it; contend for it; pray fervently for it: "He is a rewarder of those who diligently seek Him" (Hebrews 11:6). If you sense that it's time to move one, I still suggest waiting, contending, and praying. This question does not have a one-size-fits-all approach. From my experience, most move forward too soon because they are in a hurry to meet someone new. We must slow down so we don't zoom past God's will. He will lead but in His time. Most of us rush ahead ... we either miss companionship and sex, or we hear the biological clock ticking. These emotions end up controlling our decisions rather than allowing patience to run its course.

Although many are divided on the issue of divorce and re-marriage, one thing is certain: God will direct those who commit their lives completely to Him, this we know. This brief section is written primarily to those on the "receiving" end, who by no choice of their own, are separated or divorced, and are uncertain... should they hold on for restoration, or move on. Before making any decision of this magnitude, I offer three directives.

1. First, discontinue any relationship that is not God-centered, or that seems to cloud your judgment. Re-bound relationships are often not God's will. Sadly, countless marriages are never restored simply because of immediate involvements in other relationships. They don't wait on the Lord. I cannot stress this point enough.

2. Second, pray, seek godly counsel, and allow God's Word to direct you. However, another word of caution here: don't look for people who will tell you want you want to hear; seek godly men or women who can offer wise counsel. Even with that, counsel should not direct, they should only confirm. All destructive relationships, bad advice, and toxic influences must be severed as you seek direction. The alarming divorce rate leaves one to wonder who's guiding Christians today—the flesh or the Spirit?

3. Third, again, don't be in a hurry. "Those who wait upon the Lord shall renew their strength" (Isaiah 40:31). Restoration is a process. Don't abort the process because you're in a hurry. Healing and waiting on the Lord require time and patience. If it took years to damage the marriage, it may take time to rebuild... or for emotional wholeness

to be restored. I have witnessed many couples give up on their marriage simply because restoration did not happen in their time-frame and according to their plan.

As stated earlier, one of the most difficult Scriptures dealing with divorce or separation is found in 1 Corinthians 7:10-11, "To the married I give this charge (not I, but the Lord): the wife should not separate from her husband (but if she does, she should remain unmarried or else be reconciled to her husband), and the husband should not divorce his wife." This clearly states that those who are divorced and/or separated, unless "scripturally released," should not remarry. And even in cases where one is scripturally released, the heart of God may be one of forgiveness and reconciliation.

If this verse applies to your situation, it's wise to allow a significant amount of time to pass before considering re-marriage. Time reveals if the spouse left only for a season, or has chosen to leave permanently. **We should turn to the Scriptures for direction, not look for loopholes.**

1 Corinthians 7:15 says that a Christian is "not under bondage" if an unbeliever leaves. When a spouse leaves and has moved on with no intention of returning, God does not want the other spouse to be bound to the past— He wants us to live in peace. But does this mean that the abandoned spouse is now free to remarry? Again, theologians are divided on this issue, but, in my opinion, the word "bondage" (douloo) is the key. If an unbelieving spouse leaves and ends the marriage, the other is released

and is free to remarry. They are no longer a slave; they are released.

As a practical example, many happily married people would be forever single if they took this verse to mean that they are prohibited from ever remarrying. They would not have a new loving spouse and wonderful children. This, to me, would be true bondage. But "I say this as a concession, not as a command" (1 Corinthians 7:6). Many commentaries discuss the theological issues surrounding divorce and remarriage, but they often fail to provide a roadmap through the painful emotional toll that it takes on the family, as well as the individual.

On the flip side, what if the spouse who left is a believer? An entire book could be written on this, but suffice it to say that serious consideration must be taken here. Some spouses leave because the environment is unbearable, not because they are an unbeliever.

Let me take this opportunity to speak to the Christian who had no solid scriptural grounds for divorce, yet chose to leave. Matthew 19:9 states that a person who divorces his spouse and marries another person commits adultery, unless the spouse has been unfaithful. This is serious business. We would not intentionally walk into the enemy's camp, yet this is what we do when we walk out from under God's covering. The choices we make today will influence the quality of our life tomorrow. Sin takes us farther than we want to go, keeps us longer than we want to stay, and costs us more than we want to pay. God can restore your life, and in some cases, your marriage. If you have sinned in this area, repent and seek God again. He will forgive you ... this we know. If restoration is possible, contend for it, but if you or your spouse has remarried, don't live with on-going regret. The heart of God is that repentance and forgiveness take place even if restoration does not.

Clearly, a spouse who has been unfaithful releases the other and the faithful spouse is no longer bound. It is unfortunate that all divorced individuals are referred to as "divorced"—it would be helpful and less confusing for those whose spouse was unfaithful to be referred to as "released." However, unfaithfulness does not mean that the marriage cannot be restored if both the husband and wife seek God's guidance.

On a closing note, understand that you cannot control the choices that others make. You may be able to influence them or encourage them, but ultimately the choice to leave or to stay is up to them. They are responsible for their actions ... not you. God has given us the freedom to choose, and in marriage the choices of one will affect the life of the other.

A personal favorite, 1 Corinthians 7:17 states that we must accept whatever situation the Lord has put us in, and continue on as when God first called us. We are to use every situation for God's glory. If single, use that opportunity to build and strengthen character, and care for the things of God. If separated, use that time to seek God more fervently and pray for guidance, direction, and restoration. Allow Him to mold and direct you, and rebuild the relationship, if that's still an option. If divorced, use that experience to learn while asking God what good can come from it. Your marriage may be restored or maybe you'll minister to others who have gone through a divorce. God uses our brokenness to help others. In fact, it is in our weakness that His strength is manifested. Be assured that all things work together for good as we commit our lives to Him!

**Granted, life will seem unclear and confusing at times, but God promises that He will guide you.** As stated earlier, don't let discouragement and failure stand in your way. I could write an entire book on my failures, but instead, I strive to follow the Apostle Paul's advice and I encourage you to do the same: Forget about those things that are behind you. Instead, reach forward to those things that are ahead of you (cf. Philippians 3:13). Forget your past mistakes, but remember the lessons learned because of them.

## EBook Sermon Links:

1. Divorce—Hope for the Hurting: https://vimeo.com/39250214

2. He Shall Direct Your Path: https://vimeo.com/50679753

3. Help! My Life isn't Working: https://vimeo.com/57997410

4. Changed—God Takes Nothing and Makes Something: https://vimeo.com/64176026

# CHAPTER SEVEN: Group Study Questions

1. Recall the two women from the opening of the chapter—regardless of what they had endured, God delivered them from emotional scares and feelings of abandonment. How can He deliver you as well?

2. God can turn brokenness into an unbreakable force, but it is imperative that your mind is renewed by applying biblical principles, beginning with forgiveness. Are there any areas in your life that require forgiveness?

3. Comment on 1 Corinthians 7:10-11, "A wife must not leave her husband. But if she does leave him, let her remain single or else go back to him. And the husband must not leave the wife."

4. A consistent theme throughout the Bible is: hearing plus doing equals success. How can this lead to restoration in many cases? Are there any areas where you are not obeying God?

5. Clearly, a spouse who has been unfaithful releases the other and they are no longer bound, but how can a person still find hope in God? When is restoration possible? List examples.

# Health—Don't Overlook This Area

"My children are over-weight. The oldest was just diagnosed with diabetes. My poor health is also taking a toll on me. Help!"

*A concerned mother*

Although I believed I was healthy and fit, by the time I reached my twenty-second birthday, my 6'2" frame had skyrocketed to 270 pounds and I was diagnosed with borderline hypoglycemia. My blood pressure and my cholesterol levels were high, my health was rapidly deteriorating. I was told that I might need to take medication for the rest of my life. As a result, I was denied life insurance and was instructed by my physician to "go on a strict diet." I was shocked! I knew that if I didn't change my life, my life would change me!

I immediately drove to a bookstore and purchased a diet book convinced that it would help. It worked, but only temporarily. Within a few months, I gained back all the weight I had lost. I continued to try different diets for several more years; all of them failed miserably. As a result, I became angry and frustrated. *Many of the diets presented what I wanted to hear, and not what I needed to hear to live a healthy life.* It shouldn't be about selling products, pills, and false promises, the truth is enough. The truth is that we are losing the war against obesity and poor health. And unless we change the way we approach this topic it will not improve.

Between 1992 and 2000, I was an employee, then a manager, and finally a corporate executive in Southern California for the fastest growing fitness company in the world at that time. I managed fitness centers and personal training departments while assisting and interviewing thousands of weight-loss clients. As a result, I identified a consistent pattern that surfaced time and time again: those who were fit rarely, if ever, referred to "dieting," while those trying to lose weight often referred to being on a "diet." Those who were fit, whether they knew it or not, often followed a biblical plan; they didn't diet. I applied these principles in overcoming my own health and weight-loss challenge.

During this time in the health and fitness industry, God radically changed my life. While I had focused on prosperity, wealth, and success, I had starved my soul. I tried everything that the world had to offer, but ultimately, I found that it offered little of lasting value. God used this time to bring the prodigal son home. I resigned from my position in 2000 and began working on my first book, *What Works When "Diets" Don't.* Although my theological foundation was still developing (I would definitely reword and/or delete some of the content in my first few books), this book was a very helpful resource for those seeking optimal health. I will cover some of that information in this chapter because I believe that physical health often runs parallel with spiritual health. It should never be our primary focus—spiritual health is vitally more important (cf. 1 Timothy 4:8). But physical health should not be overlooked. **When we are healthy and fit, we are often ten times for effective, but when we are sluggish and overweight energy is diminished.** Not to mention the impact that our lifestyle has on our children.

I'm deeply saddened by the number of people who neglect their health as if it doesn't matter to God. Life is a gift; our body is the only place we have to live. This is why I included this chapter. Although we've discussed the health of our spirit and soul, little has been said about our physical health; therefore, it's time to shift gears.

The physical health of our body plays a large role in our overall health—mentally, emotionally, and spiritually—the overall quality of life improves significantly. Taking care of the one body that God has given us is wise stewardship... it affect our entire life. Although spiritual health is first and foremost, our physical health also plays a vital role in productivity. According to many experts, many diseases are preventable through proper nutrition and exercise. To suggest that health should not be a priority is to suggest that God isn't concerned with this area.

It's ironic... we have more fitness centers, more personal trainers, more books, and more articles written about fitness than ever before, yet health-related illnesses and problems caused from poor nutrition and obesity are increasing at an alarming rate. We pray for healing, but often neglect the primary cause of disease—poor health. It reminds me of the man who prayed, *"Lord, please increase my finances ... my debt is killing me,"* as he headed to Las Vegas with his weekly check.

Granted, I don't believe that everyone will be healthy and wealthy. We live in a very sinful world that often results in disease and sickness. **God sometimes uses pain, sickness, disease, and suffering to draw us closer to Him; however, we cannot throw the baby out with the bathwater and totally dismiss physical health.** Obesity and poor health zaps energy and robs from life. Poor nutrition affects us negatively in several different ways. High levels of caffeine or nicotine, for example, lead to irritation, anger, impatience, and anxiety... not good qualities to possess. They are the exact opposite of the fruit of the Spirit. As a side note, the majority of people I've counseled who damage their family through anger are often addicted to caffeine, nicotine, alcohol, drugs, and so on. Clearly, health plays a vital role in our overall attitude. When we feed the body what it needs, it will run better.

I also encourage those suffering with depression and anxiety to look first at their spiritual and physical health. I'm not minimizing depression or anxiety, they are debilitating, but we shouldn't immediately assume that we need a prescription without first checking the obvious—do we have a strong devotional and prayer life, are we monitoring our thought life and media choices carefully, are we taking care of our body? Exercise is a natural stress reliever. God created us to move and to be active. Regardless of what the culture promotes, choosing to follow a healthier lifestyle is the first step in making health a priority (but not an obsession).

Eating healthy is a constant challenge because temptation is always before us. The next time that you're tempted, try asking, "Does my body need it—or does it want it?" If it needs it, consume it. If it wants it, think twice. It's generally not "if" poor nutrition causes damage, but "when." What a sad commentary on the lifestyle of a nation that has such great potential to live in the blessings that God has so graciously given.

The purpose of food is to meet our nutritional needs, not our wants. That bears repeating: food was created to meet our body's "needs" not our "wants"—to heal, restore, and replenish. Many of America's most popular foods have little nutritional value, and contain harmful ingredients. Add to this the absence of organic (the way God designed it) fruit and vegetables for fiber and dietary value, and it's obvious why cancer now affects one out of three individuals—we're not feeding the body what it needs to fight cancer, heart disease, and poor health, in general. No wonder many experience extremely low energy levels, attention-deficit problems, sleep disorders, anxiety, and mood swings, to name only a few. Therefore, a first step toward better health is to eat God-given, organic foods when possible. It would have been to my benefit to follow this plan earlier in my life.

In general, the majority of diet promoters continue to focus on what we want to hear and not always on what we need to hear. They don't address the pattern between those who succeed at weight-loss and those who fail. Most offer menu plans or diet aids, but the problem is much deeper, and requires more than a quick fix. **We need a solution, not a sales pitch.**

The next step I recommend is to read food labels and to know what you're consuming. Trust me, you will be shocked. Many of the additives found in food today are simply there to enhance flavor, color, and appearance, and to substantially increase the shelf life of the product. Unfortunately, this approach is far from healthy. We were created to consume living, life-sustaining, God-given foods that nourish and support a healthy body, not dead, life-depleting food from a factory. *The life of the food is to be deposited in to the body to support and maintain life.* If you can avoid empty foods and limit caffeine and junk food consumption, and instead, consume more life-giving foods, you'll be well on your way to better health.

Another important step, although extremely difficult, involves removing addictive substances that undermine health. I vividly remember a comment from a clinical nutritionist that motivated me, "Discontinuing caffeine intake leads to significant improvements in health ... far more than just dieting alone." He also made the connection between depression, anxiety, and panic attacks to excessive caffeine.

Don't get me wrong, as a person who once loved a few strong cups of coffee, I understand that moderation is the key. However, most can't go a few days without it, they're lucky to go a few hours. Caffeine intake in the form of energy drinks, soda, tea, and coffee is highly addicted and damages health. The body is kept in a constant state of stress resulting in adrenal fatigue ... no wonder it breaks down often and why many never overcome fatigue. Contrary to popular belief, stimulants don't actually help fatigue; they contribute to it by robbing Peter to pay Paul.

**The short-term results do not outweigh the long-term damage.**

Since caffeine runs along the same biochemical pathways in the brain as cocaine, opium, and amphetamines, quitting can be a nightmare. My suggestion is to back off day by day until intake is very minimal, and use organic green tea (light caffeine) whenever possible. You'll be shocked by the results. Granted, the first week to 10-days may be torture, but it will be worth it. The withdrawal symptoms alone reveal the power of this drug. I was fascinated to read that the logo of a very popular coffee franchise represents a seductive image that allures and entices. How ironic.

Recall in an earlier chapter that the *Diagnostic and Statistical Manual for Mental Disorders* recognizes caffeine-related disorders such as caffeine intoxication, caffeine-induced anxiety disorder, and caffeine-induced sleep disorder. These can begin with even minimal doses. Increase the amount to 500mg. of caffeine (the amount found in approximately 24 ounces of coffee) and these symptoms are dramatically increased. All this can lead to angry outbursts, panic attacks, severe depression, and extreme irritability. This begs the question, "How many are suffering mentally and physically simply because of poor health—continuing the addiction rather than removing the cause of the problem?" Not in all cases, but in most, depression, anxiety, irritability, and so on, could be severely curtailed if health (spiritual and physical) was a priority.

In the same way that a hiker feels released, energized, and un-burdened after removing a 50-pound backpack, you'll feel released and energized after removing stimulants. I became a more patient, kind, and easy-going person when I quit abusing coffee. I never realized how much it was contributing to my anger, irritability, mood swings, and anxiety until at least a week after weaning off, and the withdrawals brought out the worst in me. I always excused my poor attitude with statements such as, "I had a bad day ... I'm under a lot of stress. I'm tired." Ironically, I was the primary cause of my "bad" days, stress, and fatigue. **As much as I wanted to be filled with the Spirit, I was feeding my body a substance that was counter-productive.**

Remember, your main goal is health and stimulates aren't healthy. Ask yourself, "What is the risk to my health versus the benefit to my health?" Are the benefits going to outweigh the risks? No. Your heart and organs work very hard, and they don't need added stress. As another example, some racecars are supercharged to run a quarter mile in seconds, but the engine needs to be replaced, or at least repaired, often. The same is true for your body; if you push it beyond where it's designed to go, performance won't last. The biblical approach is to take the safest route, not the fastest.

It's not my intent to point solely to coffee, stimulants, soft drinks, and energy drinks, because there are many other addictive substances; neither is being legalistic my goal. My heart is to simply share how the most addictive substance in America affects health, and then let you be the judge.

# A Biblical Approach to Health

After years of dieting, I became so frustrated that I almost gave up altogether. After all, who wants to exercise daily, follow a special diet, and sacrifice time for nothing? We want immediate results. But when the results take longer than what we had planned, we become frustrated and eventually give up. A key element of success is knowing what to expect. People succeed at health when they stop focusing on immediate results and start focusing on changing their lifestyle. **A biblical approach focuses on gradual, healthy lifestyle changes.**

It's unfortunate that we live in an age when immediate gratification has taken precedence over delayed gratification. We are told that good health can be quick and easy. As a result, we waste time and money on products that promise the world but fail to deliver worthwhile results. The majority of diet advertisers thrive on the principle that people will purchase products based on emotional response and urgency. Many have been largely conditioned to believe that they can do the least amount of work possible in the shortest amount of time where health is concerned. This is not a biblical approach. "Lose weight quick" is a great marketing slogan but it is not realistic.

I had often read that diet and energy drinks were not healthy, but that didn't stop me from consuming them on a regular basis. It wasn't until I researched the ingredients that I gave up drinking them. Not only do these beverages offer zero nutritional value, their ingredients are very harmful. Mechanics often use them to clean battery cables because of the acidic state. The heartbreaking truth is that millions of people consume these harmful ingredients on a daily basis, sometimes several times a day, without realizing what they are consuming. It's little wonder that, as a nation, we're experiencing record levels of health related problems. Again, ask yourself, "Does my body need it—or does it want it?" If it needs it, consume it. If it wants it, think twice. It's not easy to completely quit drinking these products. The media does a masterful job promoting, marketing, and winning our minds with pleasant thoughts associated with their consumption. In many cases, profit drives companies, not health!

Initially, people are highly motivated and disciplined when they begin focusing on health. Many immediately stop eating fast food, stop consuming alcohol, stop eating sweets, and start exercising excessively. But as time passes, they fail to exercise as often, they don't monitor food as closely as they once did, and they lose the motivation they once had. As a result, they fall back into old habits and behaviors, and eventually a lifestyle. But you can prevent this by introducing changes at a gradual pace and focusing on long-term results. What it takes to acquire health is what it takes to keep it. Therefore, don't attempt to change your entire lifestyle overnight. For example, cut back on sugar consumption (i.e. soft drinks and junk food) and add exercise to your daily routine a few times a week. A few weeks later, add another day of exercise and limit junk food consumption; continue until a balance is reached. Don't get frustrated. The key is to make more right choices than wrong ones. This you can begin today. **If you don't control your life, life will control you.**

Is discipline really important? Through extensive contact within the fitness industry, I found that many recognized the need for discipline but believed that they had little, if any. They conditioned themselves to believe that discipline was an attribute they could not possess. They failed to recognize that they already possessed it; identifying it was difficult. If it were possible to have offered them a generous sum of money as soon as they reached their weight-loss goal, they would have quickly become highly disciplined and lost the desired weight, simply because their motivation outweighed the obstacle. Surprising, isn't it, because health is far more valuable than money.

Case in point—almost too late for Chris:

> Chris, a fifty-four year old female, was active in her teens but an injury in her twenties set her back. She had neglected her health for several years and this pattern eventually developed into a dangerous lifestyle.
>
> She was diagnosed with high blood pressure, high triglyceride levels, and extremely low HDL levels (good cholesterol). Her doctored warned that she was a candidate for developing diabetes and other health related illnesses. At this point, she had a choice ... to encounter the pain of discipline in changing her lifestyle, or the lasting pain of regret, ill health, and a possible early death.
>
> The decision was easy. Remarkably, after forty-five days of exercise and proper nutrition, her

blood pressure and triglyceride levels dropped significantly, and the HDL count increased. Her failing health motivated her to begin. As a result, discipline increased. She didn't lack discipline— she lacked motivation.

Why do we wait? Why do you wait? Unfortunately, it took an extreme circumstance to get Chris back on track. Don't make the same mistake. Make the choice to change today and avoid the pain of regret tomorrow.

At this point in the discussion, many ask, "Do I always need to monitor caloric intake?" It can turn in to a form of dieting and an obsession, but it can also help with weight loss. It's not as necessary once you're familiar with the calorie content and nutritional value of your favorite food choices. It's all about awareness. I encourage you to chart not only for caloric awareness, but more important, for nutritional awareness. In other words, by monitoring what you eat, you can also be assured that the proper amount of fruit, vegetables, fiber, vitamins, minerals, and antioxidants are being consumed. Focus on total awareness, not just caloric awareness.

To effectively lose weight, sometimes it is necessary to be aware of how many calories you're consuming and how many you're burning in the course of a day. Some diets advise not to monitor calories. Generally, these diets tell you what to eat, when to eat, for how long, and how much. In essence, they are monitoring calories for you. But what happens when the program ends? You're on your own again. Learning how to correctly monitor caloric intake can help assure long term success.

There is a principle known as *non-exercise activity thermogenesis* (N.E.A.T.). This principle refers to the amount of energy (calories) that is burned during non-exercise activity. We see this at work when two people consume the same amount of calories over a certain period of time, one gains weight the other does not. This is generally due to *non-exercise activity thermogenesis*. For example, I had a friend who consumed as much food as I did, but over the course of a year, he weighed the same and I gained twenty pounds. This was simply due to the fact that he was more active than I was. We both exercised, but his non-exercise activity was greater than mine. This increased non-exercise activity allowed him to burn more *overall* calories. Keep this in mind when you opt to watch television rather than engage in activity. This is a biblical concept: move, serve, work, and labor. **When we are bored, we eat more and move less.**

Many of America's most popular foods have little, if any, food value, and a high calorie content. Once more, far too many people ignore the nutritional value of food. They are slowly undermining health because of poor food choices. A controversial sweetener, aspartame, for example, is used in many products (i.e., diet drinks, yogurt, gum, meal replacement drinks, supplements, etc.). Research has shown that although aspartame is sweet, the adverse effects can be very detrimental to health. It was discovered in 1965 when Dr. Schlatter, while working on an anti-ulcer medication, mixed a substance with methanol (wood alcohol). The result was a very sweet taste. The FDA has been reviewing this additive for many years and the reports have been startling. Many animals, including roaches, won't consume it. Should we? You be the judge!

Today, more than ever, we're exposed to powerful food agents, additives, and enhancers. The list of controversial products that we consume is sizeable. In all honesty, I'm surprised that we do not see more sickness and disease. Many people consume harmful foods for breakfast, lunch, and dinner, as well as snacks. For instance, how many times do people consume diet drinks or soft drinks instead of the water they need? The question isn't *if* they can cause damage to the body, but *when* they'll cause damage.

Carbohydrates are currently at the forefront of most diet discussions. They consist of foods that originate from the ground such as potatoes, whole wheat grains, fruits, vegetables, and so on, and foods developed by man. Many people choose the wrong type of carbohydrates, those developed by man: sweets, processed foods, soft drinks, pastries, white flour products, etc. Our bodies were designed to consume healthy, ground-originating carbohydrates. They are the primary source of energy. Many Scriptures found throughout the Bible make reference to carbohydrates. Ezekiel 4:9, for example, states "Also take for yourself wheat, barley, beans, lentils, millet, and spelt... and make bread for yourself." We are further encouraged to let our moderation be known to all men. The key word is *moderation*. Eat moderately and keep in mind that even healthy foods need to be consumed in moderation. When we use energy through muscle exertion and cellular activity, we must replenish the energy, often times with more carbohydrates. Carbohydrates are essential for living a healthy life.

Quick health lesson: after carbohydrates are consumed, they are broken down into glucose. One of three processes occurs: 1] the glucose serves an immediate need such as exercise or activity, or to assist in recovery, 2] if there is no immediate need, glucose (carbohydrate) is stored in the muscle and liver for future use, 3] if the liver and muscles are full, the glucose will be converted into fat and stored for future use. The storage capacity in the liver is rather small; it's used to supply energy to the brain and central nervous system, whereas, the storage capacity in the muscle is larger (more muscle means more storage capacity). Weight gain occurs when too many calories are consumed and not used. Protein that should be used for building and repairing muscle is instead being used for energy due to the lack of available carbohydrates for fuel. This is why many American's suffer from poor health—we move less and eat more.

## A Final Thought on Health

You've made the choice to change, acquired a better understanding of how your body works, and are learning to choose self-discipline over regret. Now design a plan. Having a plan is essential, but it's of no importance if you're not prepared. Prepared for what? Prepared for unseen circumstances, for illness or injury, and for the challenging but rewarding opportunities ahead. For example, when I'm sick, instead of consuming junk food, I focus on juicing organic fruits and vegetables. This not only aids in recovery, it's much easier to get back on track when health resumes.

Many who lose interest in exercising and eating correctly, do so because they are not prepared for the interruptions and the distractions that can break the routine. A successful weight-loss program will encourage you to continue, regardless of your situation. People fail at health and weight-loss not because they're defeated, but because they quit. Those who succeed are those who continue despite delays.

You might be surprised at some of the excuses I've heard throughout the years in the fitness industry, but I'm sure you won't be surprised to learn that *TIME* is the number one excuse, and sometimes it's a good one. Time is one of the most important commodities that you possess. It can thrust you into the core of achievement or it can leave you consumed with guilt and regret. Time, if left to itself, will be the thief that robs you of opportunity, but when controlled, it can be used to great advantage. Use time wisely; it cannot be replaced!

One of the most disheartening statistics about weight-loss is that a high percentage of the people who diet and lose weight, do so only to gain it back within a few years. Why is this? I've found that most depend on a short-term diet to assure long-term success. They planned a two or three month program, but, again, short-term solutions do not produce long-term results. Those who change their habits by following a realistic eating pattern and exercise program can make changes that last a lifetime. As your body adapts to these changes, the amount of weight you lose will rise and fall depending on genetic pre-disposition, lifestyle, metabolism, and the biological changes that are taking place within the body.

As we close, don't forget one major theme of this book: forget what lies behind and press ahead. Begin now initially, or begin again. Success doesn't come without failure. It's through our failures that we learn how to succeed. I want to challenge those who do have the time to eat properly and/or exercise. We often forget just how precious time is. How many days, weeks, or even months do we waste because we don't prioritize our lives? We need to be very careful when we say that we don't have enough time. What we are really saying is that it's not important. If it were important we would find the time. **If we don't schedule time, time will schedule us.** You'll never get everything done that "needs" to be done in the course of a day. Therefore, it's important to prioritize your day. Ask yourself, "What's the most important thing for me to do in any given hour?" In essence, it's all about leading a productive, balanced life, using time wisely. Don't let time be the excuse that stops you from succeeding.

As stated earlier, many of America's most popular foods have little nutritional value, and contain harmful ingredients. Add to this the absence of fruit and vegetables for fiber and dietary value, and it's obvious why cancer now affects one out of three individuals—we're not feeding the body what it needs to fight cancer, heart disease, and poor health, in general. For me, the best approach, again, is consuming God-given foods whenever possible versus foods created in a factory. **To borrow from a fellow health advisor, "If it wasn't here 100-years ago, it's probably best not to eat it."** And most of us know exactly what these are.

For those of us who eat meat, I suggest not every day, and organic whenever possible. The word "organic" is not a New Age term; it simply means that, in most cases, the food is free of pesticides, herbicides, fungicides, hormones, preservatives, sewage sludge, and so on. These things can severely damage health. Choosing organic helps avoid many toxins. It's a wonder that we don't see more disease associated with poor health. Granted, the monetary cost of healthy food is higher than processed food, but the overall cost is much lower—less sickness and fewer trips to the doctor, along with more energy and productivity; not to mention the health benefits to our children.

There is great discussion today about cancer not being able to thrive in an alkaline environment (the body's pH balance). Ironically, or should we say providentially, most God-given foods are alkaline, and thus, aid in the fight against disease; whereas junk food is often acidic and contributes to extremely poor health. God knows what He's doing. We should follow His plan.

On the flip side, we should avoid being obsessed about health and weight. Many people spend most of their lives trying to look different. They often rate their appearance by society's standard and strive to look like a "perfect ten." This false perception causes many people to remain unfulfilled, even the "tens." When we compare ourselves to others, we are not using wisdom. You were not designed to be someone else; you were masterfully designed to be you. A perfect physique does not guarantee happiness any more than a good mattress guarantees sleep. **True happiness does not come from outer appearance; it comes from spiritual health.** Although I barely scratched the surface, hopefully you will have enough information and motivation to be well on your way to better health. The following questions will help formulate a plan.

## EBook Sermon Links:

1. Myth—Fitness is not Important:
   https://vimeo.com/26328373

## CHAPTER EIGHT: Group Study Questions

1. Regardless of what the culture promotes, choosing to follow a healthier lifestyle is the first step in making health a priority. List just 3 practical examples of how you can begin. *(Mine were eating healthy, life-sustaining food as much as possible and removing high-octane stimulants. Additionally, I tried to exercise five times a week each morning.)*

2. The purpose of food is to meet our nutritional needs, not our wants. How can you begin consuming life-giving foods rather than dead foods manufactured in a factory? *(My approach was to rid my home of the majority of dead foods—out of sight out of mind.)*

3. People succeed at health when they stop focusing on immediate results and start focusing on long-term changes. What are some practical steps that you can take? *(My approach was to think long term—sports with*

*my kids as they grew, and so on. Health became a lifestyle, not a fad.)*

4. In what ways can you begin moving more? Here are some helpful hints: turn off the TV and the Internet as often as possible; serve more at church and help those in need. *(Some of my best prayer times are alone with God walking.)*

5. Many who lose interest in exercising and eating correctly, do so because they are not prepared for the interruptions and the distractions that can break the routine. How will you be different? *(I frequently take healthy snacks with me so I'm not caught off guard.)*

# How Much of God do You Want?

"I had become someone I never thought I would become. I was in complete darkness ... I would sleep in my clothes for as long as I could. I began wishing that I would die. The emotional pain was unbearable."

*Comments made "before" a man fully surrendered his life*

"I only wish that everyone could feel the love that I experienced. I'm able to forgive others and genuinely love them. I feel like I have been re-born ... elusive peace has now been found."

*Comments made "after" he fully surrendered his life*

"I would like to buy three dollars worth of God, please. Not enough to explode my soul or disturb my sleep, but just enough to equal a cup of warm milk, or a snooze in the sunshine ... I want ecstasy, not transformation. I want the warmth of the womb, not a new birth. I want a pound of the eternal in a paper sack. I would like to buy three pounds of God, please" (Wilbur Reese).

Recall what I wrote in the introduction, that one of the most difficult challenges associated with pastoring is not sermon preparation, leading a church, or taxing counseling appointments; it's witnessing the tragic results of spiritual dehydration—watching people die spiritually with living water just steps away. Most are not *Desperate for More of God*. Sadly, we are too busy and too self-absorbed to drink of the living water of which Christ often spoke. The excuses are broad, the solution is narrow: "Whoever drinks the water I give him will never thirst" (John 4:14). Very few are truly hungry and thirsty for God.

In today's culture, there are countless enticements that pull us away from a fully surrendered life. It is my firm belief that, second only to salvation, the fully surrendered life is the most important aspect of the Christian life ... to truly know God: "You will seek me and find me when you seek me with all your heart" (Jeremiah 29:13). Very few of us ever experience this close relationship with God. The fully surrendered life involves things such as humility, dying to self, vibrant prayer, and heart-felt worship. This isn't meant to discourage, but to convict. Conviction is a wonderful gift from God used to turn the heart back to Him.

**The Puritans used the phrase, "The same sun that melts the wax hardens the clay."** In the same way, we can allow the Word of God to soften our hearts, or we can resist and become hard as stone. Let's be honest: how many can truly say like Jeremiah, "His word is in my heart like a fire, a fire shut up in my bones. I am weary of holding it in; indeed, I cannot" (Jeremiah 20:9)? How many have truly experienced Jesus' words in John 7:38,

"Whoever believes in me, as the Scripture has said, out of his heart will flow rivers of living water?" How many can truly relate to "times of refreshing" found in Acts 3:19? How many really understand the words of John the Baptist when he cried out, "After me will come one who is more powerful than I, whose sandals I am not fit to carry. He will baptize you with the Holy Spirit and with fire" (Matthew 3:11)? Many have head knowledge, but they've never truly experienced the presence of God.

On New Year's Eve 2011, I spent some time alone in a cabin to slow down, reflect, and pray—to renew my mind. The importance of time alone with God is invaluable. Renewal begins and ends with prayer. To renew means "to reestablish something after an interruption." Life can easily interrupt fellowship with God. We are renewed through prayer and time alone with Him—mighty fillings of the Spirit often occur after extended times of prayer.

During this private time of revival, I was reminded that the overall spiritual condition of *Westside Christian Fellowship* will be a reflection of my prayer life. E.M. Bounds believed that without prayer in the pulpit, "The church becomes a graveyard, not an embattled army. Praise and prayer are stifled; worship is dead. The preacher and the preaching encourage sin, not holiness ... preaching which kills is prayerless preaching. Without prayer, the preacher creates death, and not life."[21] You may ask, "What does this have to do with me; I'm not a pastor?" Everything! Prayer moves the hand of God. The same could be said about your home. The overall spiritual condition of your family will be a reflection of your prayer life. The fully surrendered life and prayer go hand-in-hand.

Moses spent time on the backside of the desert before leading Israel out of bondage. Elijah heard the still small voice of God alone in a cave. Jacob wrestled with God in the stillness of the night and his name was changed to Israel. John the Baptist lived alone in constant prayer with God. Jesus often retreated to isolated places for extended times of prayer. How then are we to lead the church, and our families, in these dire times if we do not cultivate a strong prayer life? The depth of our relationship with God is in direct proportion to the depth of our prayer life. Prayer matters. The fully surrendered life begins and ends with prayer. We must be *Desperate for More* ...

## Feed Me So I Can Destroy You

Most never experience the power of the Spirit... the power of the fully surrendered life, because of idolatry. Our idols knock and we open the door. Commentator, Klyne Snodgrass, states it well, "Mention of the 'schemes' of the devil reminds us of the trickery by which evil and temptation present themselves in our lives. Evil rarely looks evil until it accomplishes its goal; it gains entrance by appearing attractive, desirable, and perfectly legitimate. It is a baited and camouflaged trap."[22] **It's often not until after sin has accomplished its purpose that we see its destructive path.** Only by comparing thoughts and actions to God's Word can we have the insight to see beyond the circumstances.

Being tempted isn't sin—surrendering to it is. Temptation is also an opportunity to do what is right by turning from it. 1 Corinthians 10:13 states, "No temptation has overtaken you except such as is common to man; but God is faithful, who will not allow you to be tempted beyond what you are able, but with the temptation will also make the way of escape, that you may be able to bear it." This "way of escape" is ultimately what tilts the scale toward the fully surrendered life. When we flee temptation, turn from sin, and seek God, the by-product is the filling of the Spirit. The door of temptation swings both ways—you can enter or exit. If we choose to enter, once inside, we may not see the exit sign so clearly again.

This entire book was written to encourage the filling of the Spirit (cf. Ephesians 5:18). The Spirit-filled life is really about choices. Do our choices quench and grieve the Spirit, or do they foster growth? Consider these points:

- *The flesh is in rebellion against God.* Puritan author, John Owen, writes, "Secret lusts lie lurking in your own heart which will never give up until they are either destroyed or satisfied."[23] The flesh—although it feels comfortable and natural at times—is not a friend to be trusted. "The carnal mind is enmity against God" (Romans 8:7). Enmity is not just an enemy, an enemy can be reconciled; enmity is in direct opposition to God. In short, the flesh says, "Feed me so I can destroy you... destroy your health, your relationships, your soul." C.H. Spurgeon warned, "Beware of no man more than of yourself; we carry our worst enemies within us."[24]

229

- **The devil doesn't make us do anything he simply presents the bait.** For example, the devil doesn't show a young couple the pain and anguish and the years of regret that premarital sex brings; he deceives them with temporary enjoyment and a false sense of freedom from responsibility. He has been deceiving since the beginning of time. When the woman in Genesis 3:6 saw that the fruit of the tree was good and pleasing to the eye, and also desirable for gaining wisdom like God, she gave into the temptation (took the bait) and rejected God's Word. She also gave some to her husband and he ate. Nothing has changed. The devil still presents the bait, but instead of taking responsibility for actions, many blame the devil for their poor choices. "The devil is coming after my finances," they say; yet they fail to budget, give, and spend wisely. "The devil is trying to destroy my marriage," is another common statement; yet spouses fail to truly love and serve one another.

Although the enemy will come against our family and our finances, we cannot blame him... we must take responsibility for our poor choices when warranted. According to 1 John 2:16, we are drawn away through the lust of the flesh (unbridled passions), the lust of the eyes (covetousness), and the pride of life (boasting in what we have and/or do). The first step toward victory is to take responsibility for our actions, submit them to God, and resist the devil: "Submit yourselves therefore to God. Resist the devil, and he will flee from you" (James 4:7).

- **Be aware of "opportune times."** Luke 4:13 says, "And when the devil had ended every temptation, he departed from him until an opportune time." In battle, the enemy attacks at opportune times. "Opportune times" in the Greek language denote a favorable wind blowing a ship toward its destination. The world entices through cravings for physical pleasure and through covetousness, and through pride in our achievements and possessions. These are the three areas where the enemy will concentrate his focus; be aware of these "opportune times."

- *The source of our strength comes from the food that we choose.* What we feed grows, and what grows becomes the strong and dominating force within our lives. Our thoughts become words, our words become actions, our actions become habits. Who is shaping your thoughts? A daily diet of violence, lust, anger, and depression will fuel those very things in your life. Again, the devil doesn't make us do anything; he simply presents the bait. James 1:14-15 says that each one of us is tempted when we are drawn away by our own evil desires. Then, after the desire has been acted out, it gives birth to sin; and sin, when it is full-grown, leads to death (e.g. feed me so I can destroy you).

In closing this section, be encouraged. When you truly seek God's help, you can overcome temptation instead of allowing temptation to overcome you. The key is to pray for strength and wisdom, and to be mindful of the warfare and the weapons of warfare (see Ephesians 6), and then choose accordingly. When we yield to temptation, we walk willingly into the enemy's camp and quench and grieve the Spirit within us. *An immediate full turn in the opposite direction at the first sign of temptation will encourage victory.*

Temptation also comes in the form of ungodly relationships. We can be easily misled when we allow bad company to corrupt good character (cf. 1 Corinthians 15:33). *Whom we associate with may be who we become.* Choose friends and relationships wisely. From time to time, you may feel helpless and depressed even when you're doing all you know to do. You may even feel like giving up and returning to your familiar comfort zone. DONT! This thinking is wrong. Press through. You are exercising the very important spiritual muscle called perseverance. There is a saying that ships are safest in the harbor, but they are not made for the harbor. Likewise, you were designed to weather storms successfully. When life becomes difficult and challenging, set your sites on the goal not on the challenge. As a believer, you were not created to fail, you were created to succeed. There is often a blessing just beyond the circumstance. Simply trust despite appearances and keep moving forward.

## The Price and Power of Revival

Duncan Campbell, in his book, *The Price and Power of Revival,* makes a very compelling point:

> **"How is it that while we make such great claims for the power of the Gospel, we see so little of the supernatural in operation?** Is there any reason why the Church today cannot everywhere equal the Church at Pentecost? I feel

this is a question we ought to face with an open mind and an honest heart. What did the early Church have that we do not possess today? Nothing but the Holy Spirit; nothing but the power of God. Here I would suggest that one of the main secrets of success in the early Church lay in the fact that the early believers believed in unction from on high and not entertainment from men .... How did the early Church get the people? By publicity projects, by bills, by posters, by parades, by pictures? No! The people were arrested and drawn together and brought into vital relationship with God, not by sounds from men, but by sounds from heaven .... The early Church cried for unction and not for entertainment. Unction is the dire and desperate need of the ministry today."[25]

I couldn't agree more with Mr. Campbell's perspective.

George Watson adds, "The true saints of God, who have clear heads, and pure, warm hearts, have in all generations had to walk between the two extremes of cold formality on the one side, and wild, ranting fanaticism on the other. Dead formality and the false fire of fanaticism are both Satan's counterfeits, and he does not care into which extreme the soul plunges...".[26]

Watson masterfully describes how God's Spirit can be suppressed or misrepresented. To clarify, the Holy Spirit is not some weird, mystical force. He is part of the triune nature of God. The Bible says that the Spirit intercedes, leads, guides, teaches, and so on (cf. Romans 8:26; Acts

8:29; John 16:13). He enables and empowers us to hunger and thirst for righteousness, and to boldly live for Christ. God's Word becomes living and active in the life of the believer who is continually filled with the Holy Spirit. **Charles Spurgeon adds, "What can a hammer do without the hand that grasps it, and what can we do without the Spirit of God?"**[27]

By age 28, my life was filled with what the world offered, but I was empty inside. I was at a turning point. I could choose to turn to God or continue to reject Him. By God's grace, I repented and put my complete trust in Christ. Although far from perfect, God radically transformed and redirected my life through the power of the Holy Spirit. He can do the same for you. Acts 1:8 identifies this experience: "You shall receive power when the Holy Spirit has come upon you; and you shall be witnesses." The power of the Holy Spirit is like dynamite that ignites a hunger for God so intense that every aspect of life is changed—we become bold not passive, stable not fanatical, and committed not wavering.

Within the months that followed this experience my passion and purpose for life became clearer than ever. I then understood Acts 3:19, "Repent therefore and be converted, that your sins may be blotted out, so that times of refreshing [revival] may come from the presence of the Lord." I truly experienced this infilling of the Spirit that is seen throughout the Scriptures (e.g., a transformed life resulting in a love for God and His Word). From this experience, came books, articles, speaking engagements, and ultimately, a church.

I, like many Christians, tend to be "safely" conservative when considering the power of the Holy Spirit; however, Scripture clearly supports the miraculous work of the Spirit today. I'm open but cautious. We need sound doctrine and the power of the Holy Spirit. As I said earlier, it is possible to be "Bible taught," but not "Spirit led"—straight as a gun barrel theologically, but just as empty. The letter kills, but the Spirit gives life (cf. 2 Corinthians 3:6). Don't get me wrong, theological and expositional teachings are essential to Christian living, but how often are theology students encouraged to fast and pray as well as study? How often are they taught brokenness and repentance in addition to translating the Greek language? How often are they taught the surrendered life? **We can sometimes be more concerned about a Master's Degree than a degree from the Master.**

The Holy Spirit inspired the Scriptures and empowered Jesus and the Apostles. We are desperately remiss if we fail to recognize His vital role in our lives. "We need to close every church in the land for one Sunday and cease listening to a man so we can hear the groan of the Spirit which we in our lush pews have forgotten" (Leonard Ravenhill). Granted, we have gifted leaders who are led by the Spirit, but we, individually, need to spend serious time searching and listening to God.

Sadly, we often pray on the run and scurry through a 5-minute devotional, yet we devote hours to television, movies, and the Internet, and we wonder why we know little of the power of the Spirit. Recall R.A. Torrey's words, "We must spend much time on our knees before God if we are to continue in the power of the Holy Spirit." The only thing holding many churches together today is social activity, not the activity of the Spirit. A.W. Tozer insightfully said, "If the Lord's people were only half as eager to be filled with the Spirit as they are to prove that they cannot be filled, the church would be crowded out." *I sincerely believe that the greatest need in the church today is to confess our sins, pray often, obey the Word, and be filled with the Spirit.*

## The Key—Avoid Extremes

Christians can embrace one of two extremes concerning the word "revival." At one extreme are those who embrace pure emotionalism and hysteria—"if it's odd it's God"—all weird behavior is excused. The other extreme lacks a living, vibrant spiritual life. The church feels dead, cold, and lifeless. Talk of reviving the things of God (revival) is either dismissed or ridiculed. **Both extremes can hinder the work of the Holy Spirit and genuine Christian growth.** I will primarily address the first extreme where I have viewed videos of people supposedly "getting high," "toking," and "drunk" on the Holy Ghost. This is not the same as being filled with the Spirit of God (cf. Ephesians 5:18). I have seen video footage of people being led around like dogs on a leash and acting like animals. Yes, I'm serious... bizarre and grossly unbiblical manifestations are not reflective of one filled with the Spirit. Those truly filled with the Spirit reflect the personality and nature of God.

When questioned about extremes in this type of odd behavior, there are no answers that find support in Scripture. Common responses are, "I know it seems bizarre, but...". Or, "I know it's weird, but...". Or, "You're quenching and grieving the Spirit by not being open." These are not biblically sound responses for such bizarre manifestations. The Holy Spirit is not quenched when we honor God's Word and "test the spirits, whether they are of God" (1 John 4:1). He is quenched and grieved when we do not test and discern—when we allow the Holy Spirit to be misrepresented. The apostle Paul, in 1 Corinthians 2:15, said that we are to judge, or discern, all things. **Someone truly filled with the Spirit though bold, is often not bizarre.**

Scriptures are often used in an attempt to support very odd behavior. For example, Acts 2:15 states, "For these are not drunk, as you suppose, since it is only the third hour of the day," and John 18:6 records that men "drew back and fell to the ground" when Jesus surrendered Himself shortly before His death. These Scriptures, when used to validate wild, ranting fanaticism, are incorrect and misleading.

Granted, we cannot dismiss the truly miraculous works of God that happen daily, nor can we minimize the incredible power of God to radically change lives through the power of the Spirit. However, in our zeal and excitement we often minimize the need for discernment. A discerning person considers supernatural experiences in light of God's Word, nature, and character. They ask, "Is there genuine fruit? Does the experience align with God's Word? Is the fruit of the Spirit found in Galatians 5 present: love, joy, peace, long-suffering, kindness, goodness, faithfulness, gentleness, and self-control?" A true, genuine experience with the Holy Spirit will produce godly fruit and obedience to God. It seeks to promote those things that are pure and righteous. A word of caution here: even those in the New Age movement experience powerful feelings of love and euphoria, but it doesn't draw them closer to Christ or lead to repentance or surrender to the true God.

Although sincere, we can be sincerely wrong and seriously misled. **Having an experience or being enlightened can create "feel good" emotions, but it does not necessarily mean that it is right.** *Even though there is flexibility and freedom, our experiences must align with the Scriptures and the character of God.* "We should not interpret Scripture in the light of our experiences, but rather, interpret our experiences in the penetrating light of Scripture" (D. Martyn Lloyd-Jones).[28] Feelings can be good and God-given; however, we cannot forget the prophet Jeremiah's words, "The heart is deceitful above all things, and desperately wicked; who can know it?" (17:9). Profoundly moving experiences do stir emotions, and they may "feel" right; however, emotions are primarily a vehicle for expression, not a gauge for truth.

Sadly, some of the disturbing behavior mentioned earlier has been excused, and some of the leaders of these movements are rarely challenged. They can divorce their spouses and remain in leadership using 1 Chronicles 16:22 as a proof text, "Do not touch My anointed ones, and do My prophets no harm." This is an abuse of grace at the highest level and a twisting of Scripture. We should forgive, but reinstatement raises several questions. In our zeal to defend the Holy Spirit, we sometimes run the risk of defending wrong behavior. *One can rise to the top because of ability, but plummet to the bottom because he or she lacks spiritual character.* Throughout the Old Testament, God gave people the opportunity to be leaders, but it was their character and their humility, not their position, that determined their outcome.

To counter this criticism, some of the followers of this movement say that those who oppose them will suffer the judgment of God, when, in reality, it is those who refuse God's offer of salvation who will suffer judgment. **A person is not judged for seeking discernment, they are judged for rejecting the truth (cf. Romans 1:18).**

Although some well intentioned Christians are anxious to hear from God, many seek signs and wonders rather than seeking the Lord. We can become unstable, confused, and deceived when spirituality hinges only on signs, wonders, and manifestations. Instead, seek first the kingdom of God and His righteousness and everything else will fall in place (cf. Matthew 6:33).

Please understand, it's not my intention to paint experience-oriented movements with a broad brush—God wants us to experience Him. The presence and the power of the Holy Spirit can provoke overwhelming feelings, and rightly so. When truth penetrates the heart, excitement, passion, and enthusiasm often follow. These emotions can be good and God-given. *My goal is not to limit the gifts, power, and presence of the Spirit, but to seek balance and discernment.*

One of the reasons why people embrace unbiblical experiences is because they are not in the Word seeking balance, confirmation, and discernment. Simply stated, if we are not in the Word, the Word will not be in us. We can easily be deceived. **Searching for spiritual fulfillment isn't wrong, but where we search can be.** Spiritual hunger is good, yet we can be so hungry spiritually that we'll consume anything. Eagerness to consume can lead to "experience" oriented movements with no scriptural basis, especially when we begin to look to experiences to validate truth. God is working whether we "feel" something or not.

Some of the events where oddities occur can feed sinful desires rather than challenge them. Granted, there are those who attend these events who are truly seeking God. I'm not minimizing that; I applaud them for seeking, but the "signs and wonders" gospel is not the real gospel, nor is the "prosperity gospel" the real gospel. God may prosper us, and miracles do happen, but these are secondary—Christ is primary. Many godly people do not experience great prosperity, which can be a blessing because riches often draw us away from God. The greatest miracle is that God saved us and now calls us to help others.

Granted, Christians can look odd to the culture, and God is not predictable, but this is not what I'm referring to. Again, I'm referring to bizarre occurrences such as people appearing drunk at the pulpit, toking the Holy Ghost, acting like animals, and screaming as if they were on fire. Can we honestly believe that Jesus, Peter, and Paul would endorse, or worse yet, partake in weird behavior?

The Apostle Paul warns against confusing and immature behavior that compromises the gospel. *Falsehood and confusion often go hand-in-hand.* Paul often corrected err in his epistles, and in 1 Corinthians 14:40 he concludes, "Let all things be done decently and in order." Rather than quenching and grieving the Spirit, Paul is pleading for sound action and for decency and order within the church when possible. The church is to be "the pillar and ground of the truth" (cf. 1 Timothy 3:14-15).

There are incidences of odd behavior in the Bible, such as the man from the country of the Gadarenes who was possessed, but after He met Jesus he was "sitting at the feet of Jesus, clothed and in his right mind" (Luke 8:35). We also have an account of a man who brought his possessed son to Jesus: "And as he was still coming, the demon threw him down and convulsed him. Then Jesus rebuked the unclean spirit, healed the child, and gave him back to his father" (Luke 9:42). In these cases, very odd behavior is the result of people needing Christ. His presence and deliverance brings peace and order.

As a student of revivals, I understand that being "controversial" isn't necessarily a bad thing. Again, God is not predictable, and odd things can happen when sinful man is overcome by the power of God. As I read the Journals of George Whitefield, the Welsh Revivals, and the first hand accounts of the First Great Awakening in America, I found that Pastor Jonathan Edward's words were true. He observed that a work of the Holy Spirit would be evident: 1) it would elevate the truth, 2) exalt Christ, 3) oppose Satan, 4) point people to the Scriptures, and 5) result in love for God and others. The focus was on preaching the totality of God's Word, calling out sin, and correcting err—holiness is sought, not hysteria. **The result is genuine fruit, not ungodly fanaticism.**

Some suggest that today's battle is not so much against liberals in the church, but against those who are "not open" to new prophecies and visions—those who "religiously hold to the written Word alone." This statement concerns me because it can be used to promote anything done in the name of the Lord. Granted, Acts 2:17 is relevant for us today, "And it shall come to pass in the last days, says God, that I will pour out of My Spirit on all flesh; your sons and your daughters shall prophesy, your young men shall see visions, your old men shall dream dreams." But this Scripture is balanced with, 1 John 4:1, "Beloved, do not believe every spirit, but test the spirits, whether they are of God; because many false prophets have gone out into the world." Not everything done in God's name bears His approval.

Jesus warns, "Beware of false prophets, who come to you in sheep's clothing, but inwardly they are ravenous wolves" (Matthew 7:15). There are false teachers within the church. We are encouraged to pray for wisdom and discernment. "Words from the Lord" cannot supersede the Bible, but rather, confirm it. "Prophecy involves not authoritative Bible teaching, and not speaking words of God which are equal to Scripture, but rather reporting something which God spontaneously brings to mind" (Wayne Grudem).[29] **We hold religiously to the written Word because it is our guide ... to test what is being said:** "The spirits of the prophets are subject to the prophets" (1 Corinthians 14:32).

The speaker should be careful since his words must be under, or subject to, God's Word.

A "prophet," as mentioned in the Bible, can be anyone in a position of spiritual authority or claiming to be. They are not to be elevated or idolized. We follow Christ, not men. False teachers aren't ostentatiously dressed in red, armed with a pitchfork. They often look credible and talk convincingly; however, they bring destructive teachings into the church. They tend to avoid difficult truths such as sin, judgment, and repentance, and focus on what people want to hear, rather than what they need to hear. *If those who look to the Word are accused of quenching and grieving the Spirit, we are reminded that Jesus used the Word of God for finality, discernment, and power.*

As stated earlier, false teachers provide layers of truth mixed with error, but even a broken clock is right twice a day. Today, when the truth of God's Word is spoken, people are often offended because they've been conditioned to hear "feel good" messages that do little in calling out sin. As a result, churches are filled with people whose lifestyles reflect little change. William Still said it well, "Many, who for the first time come under the sound of Holy Ghost preaching, are mortally offended ... because they have never been exposed to the white light of the Spirit."

Wisdom requires that we examine what is being sought and taught ... what is the focus? Repentance, holiness, obedience, and purity should be primary rather than boasting, blessings, abundance, and prosperity. The very thing that we need may be the very thing that we are not discussing—repentance: "The Church must first repent; then the world will break! The Church must first weep; then our altars will be filled with weeping penitents" (Leonard Ravenhill). Without holiness we will not see the Lord (cf. Hebrews 12:14).

Lastly, 2 Chronicles 7:14 is a wonderful reminder of God's call to believers, "If My people who are called by My name will humble themselves, and pray and seek My face, and turn from their wicked ways, then I will hear from heaven, and will forgive their sin and heal their land." Personal revival begins when we look in the mirror and take responsibility and turn toward God. We must be *Desperate for More ...*

## Revive our Hearts, not Heresy

Not all recent moves lack authenticity. What many have experienced are valid moves of God. Small and large revivals occurring throughout the world are truly that. While revivals may grow from pure motives and humble beginnings, they can be quenched by bizarre behavior or by leaders who lack character, or who take the glory and promote themselves. God calls us to be concerned, prayerful, and surrendered to Him.

**We easily ignore Scripture when we embrace views outside of God's revealed Word ... we default to our old nature or cultural trends, and can be easily led by false teachings.** Jeremiah 23:16 sheds even more light on the need to discern, "Thus says the LORD of hosts: 'Do not listen to the words of the prophets who prophesy to you. They make you worthless; they speak a vision of their own heart, not from the mouth of the LORD'."

We are to discern truth from error, light from darkness, and right from wrong ... but how? Jeremiah 23:17 offers one answer, "They continually say to those who despise Me, 'The LORD has said, You shall have peace;' And to everyone who walks according to the dictates of his own heart, they say, 'No evil shall come upon you'." False teachers often don't warn, confront, or convict. They offer comfortable messages and a false sense of peace, or they mislead with rules and regulations as found in 1 Timothy 4:2-3—"speaking lies in hypocrisy, having their own conscience seared with a hot iron, forbidding to marry, and commanding to abstain from foods which God created to be received with thanksgiving by those who believe and know the truth." Jesus said in Matthew 24:24 that "false Christs and false prophets will appear and deceive many." *Deception comes in many forms but centers around false hope or legalism.*

Not all leaders in experience-oriented movements are false and misleading. Many are sincere and open to the work of the Holy Spirit and understand that "experiences" cannot supersede the Word. **God's Word is the foundation on which all truth stands** (cf. 1 Timothy 3:15). What is true revival then? Simply stated, a genuine revival is God reviving His people—"Wilt thou not revive us again that thy people may rejoice in thee?" (Psalm 85:6 KJV). He fills us with joy, love, and an even greater presence of His Spirit. Repentance is often a mark of true revival. Griffith Jones, who preached during the Welsh revivals of the 18th century, records this about the "experiences" that occurred during this season of revival: "The tears [of the congregation] began to flow in streams down their cheeks. Soon, they wept openly, and cried out, 'What shall we do to be saved?'" Further, it was not uncommon for people to tremble and weep, or shout for joy under the anointed preaching of George Whitefield. Whitefield was the primary evangelist during the Great Awakening that occurred in the mid 1700s. During this time, old grudges and debts were forgiven, morality improved, many were added to the church, and there was a greater sense of the fear of the Lord. This is true revival.

Those who use past revivals to in an attempt to validate odd events today perhaps have not truly researched revivals. In reading Charismatics and Calvinists, Pentecostals and Puritans, Acts and Azusa Street, as well as countless biographies of leaders such as Martin Luther, John Calvin, John Knox, John Wesley, Robert Murray M'Cheyne, Charles Spurgeon, and D.L. Moody, and Puritans such as Thomas Goodwin, John Bunyan, John Owen, and Richard Baxter, nowhere do these leaders encourage the hysteria or the outright weirdness that we sometimes see today. Granted, there were times of strong conviction such as when people held on to trees thinking that they were falling into the abyss of hell during the famous sermon, *Sinners in the Hands of an Angry God*, by Jonathan Edwards. And people did cry out to God, and/or fall on the ground under the strong conviction of sin during the Revivals of George Whitefield, John Wesley, and Evan Roberts, but this is because sin, righteousness, and holiness were preached— "falling down on his face, he will worship God and report that God is truly among you" (1 Corinthians 14:25). This is true revival ... when man finally feels the magnitude of his sin and cries out to God.

## The Cost of Addiction

It's been said that the greatest enemy of the spirit filled life is addiction—addiction to alcohol, pornography, and drugs are obvious, but we often miss more subtle forms of addictions such as video games, work, nicotine, caffeine, social media, television, entertainment, pleasure, and so on. Please don't misunderstand, some things in moderation are fine, but when they begin to control and crowd out devotion to the Lord they hinder spiritual growth.

What if liberty turns into sin? We must repent and probably discontinue the liberty. Alcohol, for example, is a very dangerous liberty that is destroying homes and lives. I learned this lesson the hard way, even as a Christian involved in ministry. I could have a beer or two on special occasions (liberty), but because of my past problem with alcohol as a young adult, the addiction was always ready to take control again. It took an embarrassing situation for me to realize that my supposed "liberty" was really an opportunity for the enemy. I shared with my wife and a few trusted friends that I could no longer exercise this liberty. Although it might be permissible nine times out of ten, it's the tenth time that might take you down. I truly believe that abstinence should be practiced by most Christians, especially if they are in leadership. The list of men and women who have lost a great deal because of alcohol is proof enough. I have never heard anyone say that using alcohol draws them closer to God, but I have heard countless people say that it draws them away.

Take caffeine as another example. As I said before, it places the body in a "fight or flight" state; it increases anxiety, irritability, anger, hostility, and agitation. Not good. It's hard to be filled with the fruit of the Spirit such as love, joy, peace, contentment, long-suffering, gentleness, kindness, and so on when we're consuming things that promote anger, aggression, irritability, stress, anxiety, impatience, harshness, and rudeness. No wonder road rage, home rage, and all other types of rage are on the upswing. As much as I'd like to avoid this topic, I believe that it's particularly relevant. If you're not sure if you're addicted to something, just try going a few days without it; then pay attention to what you find. Moderation, or abstinence in many cases, is the key.

What about addiction to video games, work, the media, and so on? Are they drawing you away from God? Addiction, also known as "enslavement," hinders our hunger for God. Enslavement to sin must be broken. "Holiness will cost a man his sins. He must be willing to give up every habit and practice which is wrong in God's sight .... There must be no separate truce with any special sin which he loves" (J.C. Ryle).[30] Holiness has a cost but the fruit far outweighs the cost of addiction:

- THE COST: Relationship with God suffers—prayer and devotion are minimized, if not avoided.

- THE COST: The addiction fosters idolatry and prevents genuine worship. Romans 1:25 speaks of idolaters who "exchanged the truth about God for a lie" by worshipping and serving created things rather than the Creator.

- THE COST: Distance grows between our spouse and kids—we feed the addiction vs. investing time with our family.

- THE COST: Kills important relationships (isolation)— we spend time with the addiction instead of investing ourselves in others.

- THE COST: Fosters irritability and anger—we often snap and are rude.

- THE COST: Financial difficulty—overspending and poor choices feed the addiction.

- THE COST: Addiction can hinder blessings from God.

Need encouragement? Recall 1 Corinthians 10:13, "No temptation has overtaken you but such as is common to man; and God is faithful, who will not allow you to be tempted beyond what you are able, but with the temptation will provide the way of escape also, so that you will be able to endure it." The best escape route is worship. Worshipping God breaks addiction. But how? Read on ...

## Worship—the Thermometer of the Heart

"It is appropriate to ask whether there is much genuine, deep, heartfelt worship in our churches. In many evangelical churches people do not truly worship God in their hearts until the last hymn ... If genuine worship is lacking in our churches, we should ask how we can bring ourselves to experience much more of the depth and richness of worship, which is the natural response of the believing heart..." (Wayne Grudem).[31]

Dr. Grudem is correct. Many who attend church are not truly worshipping God, even though they go through the motions. But what is genuine worship? Worship is a combination of attitude and acts focused on reverence to God. The Hebrew meaning denotes a "bowing down, or prostrating oneself"; it is a posture reflecting homage and reverence toward the one true and living God. **If there is a problem with worshipping God, the problem isn't with God, the problem is with us.** Worship serves as the thermometer of the heart by measuring our spiritual condition ... are we hot, cold, or lukewarm? Granted, worship isn't necessarily measured by actions such as jumping up and down; it's measured by the condition (temperature) of our heart—is it rejoicing for joy and submitting to God?

Sadly, many confuse false worship with genuine worship. According to numerous theological resources, false worship is when an entity, person, or object is worshipped instead of God—our passion for "something" outweighs our passion for Him; it draws us away. Most don't have idols on the shelf because they are parked in the garage. We don't pay homage to a statue in the living room because we are mesmerized by a fifty inch box affectionately known as "the entertainment center." We don't sacrifice things on the altar, but we do sacrifice our time (and time with of our children) on the altar of misguided priorities. Of course cars, televisions, and the Internet are not evil, they are neutral, but it is our love for them that tilts the scale away from God. We find hours a day for entertainment, but have little time to worship. Do we honestly believe that this misapplication of priorities doesn't affect us? Think again.

False worship also includes inappropriate and improper acts supposedly directed toward God. Many simply go through the motions at church. They attend as if they are doing God a favor. The heart is not engaged and the soul is not lifted up ... they are bored. Test the spiritual condition of the heart by asking a few simple questions, "Do I want the worship time to hurry and finish? Am I dreading another song as my eyes glance at the clock? Do I come late to miss the boring worship? Is my daily routine void of worship?" If so, I would seriously encourage heart examination.

I am not suggesting that if the worship service at church seems dead and lifeless that it's our fault ... not all worship taking place is heartfelt and Spirit-led. There is dry formalism and dead ritualism taking place in the church today. Many sing "about" God but they have never truly experienced Him—head knowledge without heart knowledge. Styles of worship range from the old, beloved hymns to contemporary. An older generation may not be able to relate to the younger crowd and what they prefer and vice versa. However, all worship should be God-centered, Christ exalted, and doctrinally sound. Worship allows us to shift our focus and praise toward God.

Whether you prefer hymnals and organs or contemporary bands, is really not the issue. The issue is: are you truly worshipping God in "spirit and in truth"?

He is the Creator of heaven and earth. He is not a cosmic force, universal love, or a doting grandfather; He is the King of Kings and the Lord of Lords. We must worship Him. He created, redeemed, and saved us. As one of the countless hymns declares so well, "O' The Blood: washes me; shed for me ... what a sacrifice that saved my life, yes the blood, it is my victory!"

Luke 19:10 records, "For the Son of Man has come to seek and to save that which was lost." John 1:29 passionately declares, "Behold, the Lamb of God who takes away the sin of the world." And 1 Peter 2:24 reminds us that "He Himself bore our sins in His body on the cross." These facts demand worship. Many go ballistic when a favorite team wins, but appear handcuffed and bored in church. How sad! Worship must be a priority. This is not optional, it's vital. "I want men everywhere to lift up holy hands" (1 Timothy 2:8).

I've found that there are four primary worship blockers:

1. Men think that worship is mainly for women so they disengage. They say, "I'm just not emotional." My thought, "We express anger; is not anger an emotion? We express lust and passion for worldly pleasure; are those not emotions?" "I'm just not emotional" is an excuse designed to cover up spiritual malnutrition. **Often, we're not emotional because we are numb to the things of God ... we are not**

***Desperate for More of Him.*** Worship is measured by the condition (temperature) of our heart—is it rejoicing for joy and submitting to God? Or cold, callous, and disengaged?

2. Most don't truly know God. This is why they lack passion and a genuine relationship. A passion for God and worship are by-products of genuine faith.

3. Pride and arrogance prevent worship. In the same way that a kink in a hose prevents the flow of water, a prideful man cannot truly worship God. I'm amazed at how many people, primarily men, come late to church in order to miss the worship. Pride blocks the flow. A prideful worshipper is an oxy moron. They are too busy worshipping themselves or they are too worried about the opinions of others.

4. Our lifestyle hinders worship. We cannot live like hell all week and expect heaven to fall during worship. We cannot fill our mind with darkness all week and expect the light of Christ to shine during worship. We cannot worship ourselves and things all week and expect to turn our affections toward God on one designated day. Worship is a lifestyle! Worship and holiness are interwoven. 1 Peter 1:16 says, "Be holy, because I am holy." Again, holiness is not a strange, outdated word. Holiness is being set apart or separated from anything that causes us to sin, whether mentally (in what we think) or physically (in what we do). Holiness begins in the heart.

**There is a desperate need to preach and proclaim God's Word with genuine power if we are to**

**experience true revival and genuine worship.**
Without God's authority and power, words are lifeless.
Where are those with uncompromising power and
authority in the pulpits today? The one thing that all of the
great revivals in church history had is the one thing that
we often lack—the "genuine" power of the Holy Spirit. The
very thing that we need is the very thing that we are afraid
of. Many do not truly want revival because of fear of what
it may involve.

Sometime after planting *Westside Christian Fellowship*, I
prayed, "Lord, bring revival." I was not ready for the
response that followed. I felt impressed with these words:

> "You don't want revival—it will ruin your
> schedule, your dignity, your image, and your
> reputation as a person who is 'well balanced.'
> Men will weep throughout the congregation.
> Women will wail because of the travail of their
> own souls. Young adults will cry like children at
> the magnitude of their sin. With the strength of
> My presence, the worship team will cease
> playing. Time will seem to stand still. You won't
> be able to preach because of the emotions
> flooding your own soul. You'll struggle to find
> words, but only find tears. Even the most
> dignified and reserved among you will be broken
> and humbled as little children. The proud and self
> righteous will not be able to stand in My
> presence. **The doubter and unbeliever will
> either run for fear or fall on their knees and
> worship Me—there can be no middle**

**ground. The church will never be the same again.**"

Do you truly want genuine revival? Do you truly want to experience the Spirit-filled life? Are you really *Desperate for More of God?* Nothing will change until the answer is "Yes."

## EBook Sermon Links:

1. A Pastor's Thoughts on the Strange Fire Conference (October, 2013; also available on YouTube): https://vimeo.com/77337223

2. A Call to Worship: https://vimeo.com/56217153

3. How to be Filled with the Spirit: https://vimeo.com/67691342

4. The Holy Spirit and Fire: https://vimeo.com/67212590

5. Fasting Breaks Enslavement: https://vimeo.com/57044810

## CHAPTER NINE: Group Study Questions

1. All generations of Christians have walked between the two extremes of cold formality on the one side and fanaticism on the other. Do you agree or disagree with George Watson's statement? Is it possible to find the middle ground? How?

2. Do you tend to be "safely" conservative when considering the power of the Holy Spirit? Does Scripture support the miraculous work of the Spirit today? Explain.

3. The greatest need in the church today is to confess our sins and to be filled with the Spirit? Do you agree? Is this an area you struggle with?

4. Have you witnessed Scriptures being used to support odd behavior or sinful lifestyles? Give examples. Why is this dangerous?

5. The very thing that we need is the very thing that we are afraid of. Why aren't we experiencing revival on a broader scale personally and corporately?

# A Life Changing Experience—Do you Truly Know Him?

"I thought I had been a Christian all of my life, but your message on genuine faith really challenged me. I realized that I was not a Christian. I was living a lie."

*Online Viewer*

Some time ago, a man responded to my message and acknowledged that He wanted to be saved. I also asked if he wanted to be baptized. He said, "I'm not ready for that. I don't want to get that serious." I later found that he continued in a very destructive lifestyle and told others, "I'm not ready to give up my lifestyle."

Clearly, there was no change in this man's heart. He "wanted" to be saved but his response was superficial; it was a form of self-preservation (I don't want to go to hell). In these cases, we are motivated by what they are willing to take (heaven) rather than what they're willing to give up (sin). Numerous times when in counseling people about their need for a Savior, I've heard, "Oh, I did that already. I'm good." My question is, "Did what? How are you 'good'?" Good is never good enough. True repentance produces genuine fruit—a transformed life, a love for God and His Word, sincere humility, selfless love, true repentance, and so on.[32]

Is the direction of your heart toward God, or toward the world? Again, "Love not the world, neither the things that are in the world. If any man love the world, the love of the Father is not in him" (1 John 2:15 KJV). Sadly, we may be desensitizing our generation to the gospel by offering false assurance—the American gospel versus the real gospel. We cannot assure people of salvation minus the fruit. The American gospel says, "As long as a hand was raised or a prayer was said, you're good with God." But the Bible actually says something different. Biblical repentance involves turning from sin and turning to God—it's a condition of the heart that produces fruit. Often, it's the, "I'll give Jesus a try" attitude, rather than a broken heart desperately seeking a Savior.

Don't misunderstand: I'm not against altar calls, or raising the hand to acknowledge that a decision to follow Jesus was made ... giving anxious souls the opportunity to repent is biblical. And I'm definitely not against praying a prayer of repentance. Anytime we give an honest appeal for a person to turn to God, it's a good thing. But I am against sheer emotionalism and half-hearted considerations. In our zeal to "get people into the kingdom," we sometimes run the risk of offering false assurance. We must explain genuine repentance in light of dying to self, turning from sin, and confessing Christ as Savior and Lord. Our job is not to soften the gospel and report exaggerated numbers of conversions to impress people, our job is to lovingly and boldly proclaim the gospel in its totality and leave the results to God.

We all sin and fall short, but genuine conversion results in a broken and penitent heart (genuine fruit). John the Baptist challenged the people to "bear fruit worthy of repentance" for this very reason (cf. Luke 3:8). In counseling people who lack the fruit of conversion, I do not refer to a prayer they said, but to repentance... did it occur? Were they transformed? Prayer without repentance is like a car without an engine. It might look nice, but it's not going anywhere.

Please don't misunderstand: change is a lifelong process with many setbacks; sinners sin, but there should be some indication that a person is being transformed by the gospel. A.W. Tozer sums it up well, "It is change, not time, that turns fools into wise men and sinners into saints." Jesus said, "By their fruit you will know them" (Matthew 7:16). We must be crystal clear in explaining that salvation is a supernatural act of God that produces change. It cannot be manipulated, orchestrated, or forced.

Is it possible for people to "say" that they are Christians and still not be saved? The answer is a resounding "Yes!" In William Martin's book, *A Prophet with Honor—The Billy Graham Story*, Mr. Martin wrote of young Billy's conversion at a revival service. Martin added that although Billy was a "mental storehouse of Scripture" and "vice-president of his church's youth group [before his conversion]... he probably never imagined that he was not a Christian." But the sermon that he heard at the revival service convicted and convinced him that he had not yet truly repented and surrendered his life to Christ.[33] For young Billy, and for us, "knowing" about Jesus is not enough.

"Why a chapter on genuine faith?" you might ask. For the very reason listed above; countless people can relate to Dr. Graham's story. *Unfortunately, it's not until after a genuine conversion experience that many realize that they were never saved to begin with—they had religion but not a relationship.* It's been said that one of the greatest mission fields in the world today is the United States. This is largely because awe and respect for the Lord have been forgotten in America. There's very little brokenness and humility today. **We have turned salvation into a gimmick rather than a narrow road.** We've made Jesus a butler rather than a King. We protect self rather than die to self. We want the cross light and the road easy. "The old cross slew men; the new cross entertains them. The old cross condemned; the new cross amuses. The old cross destroyed confidence in the flesh; the new cross encourages it" (A.W. Tozer).

Titus 1:16 and James 2:14 both conclude that many people "say" that they know God, but deny Him by their lifestyle. 1 John 2:19 suggests that those who acknowledge Christ initially but deny Him later are not saved to begin with. We are reminded again of this truth in Matthew 7:22. Many will come to Jesus and say, "Lord, Lord, have we not prophesied in Your name, cast out demons in Your name, and done many wonders in Your name?" And He will say to them, "I never knew you; depart from Me, you who practice lawlessness" (7:23).

Repentance is vital to genuine faith; it changes everything. Jesus will deny a relationship with those who thought they "knew" Him. Many years ago, I applied these verses to my life: "But Lord, I attend church and pray from time-to-time, and I'm basically a good person." The answer was the same, "I don't know you." That realization transformed my life (more on this later).

Knowing "about" someone is not the same as knowing someone personally. Unfortunately, many of us who call ourselves Christians fall into this category. Matthew 7:19-21 also confirms this, "Every tree that does not bear good fruit is cut down and thrown into the fire. Therefore by their fruits you will know them. Not everyone who says to Me, 'Lord, Lord,' shall enter the kingdom of heaven, but he who does the will of My Father in heaven." What kind of fruit are you bearing?

There are times to encourage, motivate, and uplift, but there are also times to confront, challenge, and contend for genuine salvation—that time is now. The need to examine ourselves is biblical, "Examine yourselves as to whether you are in the faith. Test yourselves. Do you not know yourselves, that Jesus Christ is in you?" (2 Corinthians 13:5).

## One Word Changes Everything

As I've said before, there is a significant shift in the church today to avoid controversial truths, such as sin and repentance. God's Word says to confront, confess, and turn from sin, whereas many encourage us to ignore, overlook, and continue in it. Silence about sin minimizes the cross and makes it less offensive. The cross only makes sense in light of the consequences of sin. "To convince the world of the truth of Christianity, it must first be convinced of sin. It is only sin that renders Christ intelligible" (Andrew Murray; 1794-1866).

Many mistakenly believe that Jesus didn't mention sin—after all, He was "a friend of sinners." However, Scripture reveals quite the opposite. For example, in John 5:14 Jesus exhorted a man to sin no more or a worse thing would happen to him. He also told the woman caught in the act of adultery to "go and sin no more." In Luke 10:13-14, Jesus reprimanded cities that did not repent and turn from sin, and in the fifth chapter of Matthew He said to remove anything that causes us to sin. **It's clear that "Christ Jesus came into the world to save sinners" (1 Timothy 1:15).** Why, then, is there a move within the church to avoid mentioning sin? John 12:43 may reveal the answer, "They loved the glory that comes from man more than the glory that comes from God."

The one word that changes everything is: *repentance.* Recall the words of Richard Owen Roberts, "You can be certain that at the forefront of every significant recovery from backsliding ... the doctrine of repentance has been among the precious truths that God has quickened and used."[34] Repentance is one of the first commands in the gospel and it may be the most important word that a person hears. "Wait a minute. What about love?" Yes, thank God for John 3:16, but love doesn't nullify repentance; it encourages it—the love of God leads us to repentance.

John 10:10 says that Jesus came to give us life, freedom, and a relationship with God. Are you experiencing this abundant life? Or are you bound by sin, rules, compromise, or tradition? That can be changed: 2 Corinthians 5:17 says that if anyone is in Christ they are a new creation. The old has gone and the new is here. You must trust in Him as Lord and Savior. If you're a believer, but find yourself trapped in sin, misery, and depression, there is also hope. God's continually calls His people back to Him. If you return with all of your heart (repent), He will return to you. That's a gift of the greatest value ... a promise that will never fail.

This chapter is not promoting a works-based religion; it's demonstrating, through Scripture, the importance of having a genuine relationship with Christ—a relationship that produces godly fruit. Again, genuine faith is reflected in a transformed life, a love for God and His Word, sincere humility, selfless love, true repentance, and a disconnect from the world. Does your life reflect these characteristics? As you can see, a correct definition of repentance and genuine faith is vitally important.

Believe it or not, many within the church are seeking to replace the word "repent" with "rethink." Apparently, we need to rethink our narrow view of the gospel and our restricted view of biblical hermeneutics, so they say. This re-scripting seems ridiculous, but it's true. They argue that "repentance" may not actually mean what we think. In reality, it's no surprise that they take this position. In order for Christianity to appear palatable and less intrusive to our culture, many feel that we need to rethink, redefine, and rename difficult truths, including repentance.

Whether the word for repentance is *nocham* in the Old Testament, or *metanoeō* in the New, biblical repentance involves turning from sin and turning to God—it's a condition of the heart. Acts 3:19, that I have quoted throughout this book, unapologetically confirms this, "Repent therefore and be converted, that your sins may be blotted out, so that times of refreshing may come from the presence of the Lord." Jesus said that "unless you repent you will all likewise perish" (Luke 13:5). The influential Baptist evangelist, John R. Rice (1895-1980), said, "There is no way you can please God, no way you can have the sweet communion with Him to get your prayers answered if you are in rebellion against the known will of God." Failing to turn from sin and turn to Christ results in rebellion against God.

When Mark 6:12 records that, "they went out and preached that people should repent," Jesus wasn't suggesting that the disciples rethink their narrow-mindedness, redefine their view of sin, or reinterpret the meaning of repentance. He was saying that people need to turn from sin and turn to God. To suggest that everyone from the Old Testament prophets to Christ and the apostles, to the early church fathers and the reformers, to present day scholars and theologians, misunderstood the real meaning of repentance, is the height of arrogance and deception. I'd respect people more if they'd just say that they don't like the concept of repentance rather than trying to reinterpret its already crystal clear meaning.

Repentance is a true gift from God that affects everything in our lives. If our priorities, our passions, our goals, our dreams, and our desires are not changing—are we changing? I only say this because so many today have religion and not a true relationship with Christ. They are simply going through the motions. They have never truly repented, and thus, they lack passion for God. It's been said that if your religion has not changed your life, change your religion. Of course there are hobbies, activities, and certain friendships that will continue, but if our overall *nature* is not changing, or at least heading in that direction, we should reassess our commitment—was it genuine: did we truly repent and turn to God? Do we truly "know" Jesus Christ (relationship), or do we only know "about" Him (religion)?

"The gospel, when rightly understood and received, sets the heart against all sin" (Matthew Henry).[35] 1 John 2:15 declares, "If anyone loves the world, the love of the Father is not in him." A disobedient life should raise concerns. Recall the words of A.W. Tozer, "The idea that God will pardon a rebel who has not given up his rebellion is contrary both to the Scriptures and to common sense." (See 2 Thessalonians 1:8.) I'm aware that I'm really driving this point home, but I'd rather err on the side of speaking too much about repentance than too little.

## Keep the Course

1 John 2:3-4 says, "Now by this we know that we know Him, if we keep His commandments. He who says, 'I know Him [Christ],' and does not keep His commandments, is a liar, and the truth is not in him." The word "keep" here means *to keep watchful care of.* **In the same way that a ship's captain is committed to keep his course to**

**reach his destination, the sincerity of our commitment to Christ can be measured by how well we follow the scriptural course.** From time to time, we, like ships, will drift off course. I'm not excusing sin, but I am making a distinction between perfection and direction. Perfection is not the answer—a commitment to keep the course is. *Keep the course by loving the Lord your God with all your heart, soul, and mind; this is the greatest commandment* (Matthew 22:37-38).

Repentance is not an outdated, irrelevant word—it's a very relevant word from the heart of God. **Repentance opens the line of communication between God and man. This is the life-line for our dying world.** It's not our hold on God but rather God's hold on us that secures us. Jesus compared those who did not repent with the cities of Sodom and Gomorrah, saying that it would be more tolerable for Sodom and Gomorrah in the Day of Judgment than for those who did not repent (cf. Mark 6:7-12). No guesswork here. Again, the literal meaning of repentance is apparent throughout the Bible. How can anyone miss this? It sounds more like *eisegesis*—allowing one's ideas and opinions to interpret the Bible rather than *exegesis*—uncovering the true meaning of a passage. By redefining repentance, many are being led in the wrong direction.

Some even suggest that repentance is self-improvement or a call to fulfill our natural potential. When we repent we do improve, and our God-given potential becomes apparent, but repentance is not about self-improvement—it's about renouncing sin and turning from it. Repentance is a change of mind that leads to a change in action—brokenness, genuine sorrow over sin, and humility are marks of sincere repentance. *Lasting hope and joy are also by-products of a right relationship with God, beginning with "repentance."* This is nothing to fear but to cherish. There is always a link between genuine faith and sincere repentance.

Unfortunately, as said before, many confuse sorrow with repentance. It's possible to be sorry but not repentant. A penitent person sees sin as God sees it and turns from it. He or she does not want to continue in hurtful or harmful behavior. They accept full responsibility for their actions. At this point, tears often follow, and rightly so. The danger comes when arrogance and a hard heart prevent us from turning to God. "The proud, self-justifying, self-reliant, self-seeking self has to come simply as a lost, undone sinner, whose only hope is a justifying Savior" (Norman Grubb).[36] Take time now and ask God to help you remove those things that are hindering your relationship with Him. Genuine repentance is a life changing experience— don't run from it, run to it!

With that said, here are a few points to help keep the course:

**Sin draws us away; repentance brings us back:** "Each one is tempted when he is drawn away by his own desires and enticed. Then, when desire has conceived, it gives birth to sin; and sin, when it is full-grown, brings forth death" (James 1:14-15). Our sinful nature is at war with God. No peace treaties can be signed; no concessions can be made, sin must be aborted. "Make no provision for the flesh in regard to its lusts" (Romans 13:14). The Bible says to flee, not feed sin, to crucify, not coddle it.

***Sin brings death; repentance brings life:*** "For the wages of sin is death, but the gift of God is eternal life in Christ Jesus our Lord" (Romans 6:23). Remember that sin takes you farther than you want to go, costs you more than you want to pay, and keeps you longer than you want to stay. Sin has a tremendous price, but fortunately, this greatest of debts was paid: "The gift of God is eternal life in Christ Jesus our Lord."

***Sin separates; repentance restores:*** "Behold, the Lord's hand is not shortened, that it cannot save; nor His ear heavy, that it cannot hear. But your iniquities have separated you from your God; and your sins have hidden His face from you, so that He will not hear" (Isaiah 59:1-2). Contextually, God is dealing with the children of Israel here, but the overlapping principle applies—sin separates all nations, tribes, and tongues from God. There are two types of separation—separation from God eternally and the feeling of separation that believers experience as the result of besetting sin. If God seems distant, Bible study boring, and church inconvenient, it may be that sin is hindering your relationship with Him. Look within ... is jealousy, envy, bitterness, gossip, lust, or anger controlling your thoughts? Do you have a critical spirit? Are you compromising? Are you filled with pride and judgmentalism instead of love, joy, peace, contentment, and gentleness? If there is no repentance of besetting sin, one can never experience true freedom in Christ.

***Sin enslaves; repentance frees:*** "Do you not know that when you present yourselves to someone as slaves for obedience, you are slaves of the one whom you obey, either of sin resulting in death, or of obedience resulting in righteousness?" (Romans 6:16). Mike Wilkerson, in his book *Redemption*, writes, "Sin corrupts worship. Not a ceasing of worship but a distortion of it. We never stop worshiping. Rather, in sin, we worship anything and everything other than God. We tend to exalt a substance, an experience, a person, or a dream to the level of a god." Wilkerson continues, "We define life by its attainment, and we feel like dying when it eludes us .... The Bible calls this 'idolatry.' So addictions, for example, aren't just drug, alcohol, food, or pornography problems. They are worship disorders. They flow from hearts bent on worshiping created things rather than the Creator."[37] Sin enslaves, controls, and distorts, but repentance frees and clarifies.

As a note of great encouragement, recall that Jesus came to "save His people from their sins" (Matthew 1:22). This is cause for celebration—the penalty for sin was paid on the cross (propitiation), and our guilt was removed (expiation). Although salvation is a supernatural act of God that cannot be fully explained, Scripture offers many insights. One thing is certain: God is not wanting "any to perish but for all to come to repentance" (2 Peter 3:9).

No matter what you've done or have been through, you can accept or return to Jesus and become as new. **Again, a true measure of a person is not who they were, but who they will become.**

1. Acknowledge that you are a sinner in need of a Savior (Romans 3:23).

2. Acknowledge that Jesus died for your sins (John 3:16).

3. Repent and turn from your sins (Acts 3:19).

4. Live your life for Him (Hebrews 12:1-2).

The cross cleanses, redeems, releases, crushes, and triumphs over sin. It offers hope and peace to a dying world. "There is no peace until we see the finished work of Jesus Christ—until we can look back and see the cross of Christ between our sins" (D.L. Moody).

## EBook Sermon Links:

1. Understanding Genuine, Saving Faith [part 1 in a series of 3 messages]: https://vimeo.com/42573484

2. What Must I do to be Saved?: https://vimeo.com/63780960

3. Resurrection Life—Desperate for More: https://vimeo.com/63062756

## CHAPTER TEN Group Study Questions

1. Why would anyone seek to change the biblical definition of repentance? What would be the motive behind this type of thought?

2. Do you agree that many today have religion but not a true relationship with Christ? Why? Why not?

3. Both Jesus and John the Baptist began their ministries by preaching repentance. Does this change your view or make you think more seriously about repentance, including your own?

4. Genuine faith is reflected in a transformed life, a love for God and His Word, sincere humility, selfless love, *true repentance*, and a disconnect from the world. Do you agree? Why? Why not?

5. If you've never sincerely repented and trusted in Jesus Christ as your Lord and Savior, there is no better time than now. It's the most important decision that you'll ever make. (Check out John 3:1-21.)

# APPENDIX 1: About the Author—From Prodigal to Pastor

As a Southern California corporate executive for the fastest growing fitness company in the world in the mid-1990s, I had the opportunity to experience the devastating effects of life in the fast lane without rules or boundaries. As a result, I often went with the flow of society and focused on everything that the world had to offer.

Throughout my 20s, I continued to run from God, searching for identity and truth in everything but His Word. By age 28, I had climbed the corporate ladder. Money and success became my gods (idols) and ultimately controlled my life. I was driven but for the wrong reasons. I felt a sense of purpose but it often left me empty. I was passionate but for the wrong things. **Strength, to me, meant bench pressing over 400 pounds, drinking a 12-pack of beer, and winning most of the fights that I was in.** I failed to realize that I was weak ... I was dying spiritually. I didn't have control of my life—my life had control of me. As a result of my misguided focus, my life took several unnecessary turns for the worse. By then, alcohol, anger, and arrogance had taken their toll. My life was crumbling around me. Idols promise rewards but only bring devastation.

Depressed and desperate for direction, I began to thumb through the pages of my Bible that was shelved long ago. Two Scriptures seemed to jump from the pages: *What does it profit you to gain the whole world but lose your soul?* (Luke 9:25), and, *When you hear God's voice, do not harden your heart against Him* (Psalm 95:7-8). I suddenly realized just how far I had drifted from the truth. I was at a turning point. I could choose to humble myself and turn to God or continue to reject Him. By God's grace, I put my complete trust in Him—joy, happiness, and peace filled my heart. Within the months that followed, my passion and purpose for life became clearer than ever.

Looking back, I realize that I may have had religion but not a relationship. I lived in a Christian home, I attended a Christian school, went to a Christian church, and read the Bible and prayed from time to time, but I was confusing religion and rules with a true relationship with Christ. I would "say" that I believe in Jesus when asked, but I'm not convinced that I ever truly repented and put my trust in Him, or I may have been a prodigal. Sin confuses and distorts. I thought I was a Christian because I was basically a "good person." This is a major distinction between religion and a relationship. Religion focuses on what "we" do, but a relationship with Christ focuses solely on what "He" did.

- Religion says, "I have to follow rules." A relationship with Christ says, "Because of the price that He paid for me, I want to follow His plan."

- Religion says, "I have to go to church." A relationship with Christ says, "I want to position myself to learn more, worship Him, and benefit from fellowship."

- Religion lacks assurance, whereas a relationship with Jesus offers unfailing guidance and assurance.

- Religion is man's attempt to reach God, whereas a relationship with Christ is God reaching down to man.

Again, religion focuses on what "we" do—a relationship with Christ focuses on what "He" did. We are declared right before God when we put our trust in Christ not in our "good" works. This is often referred to as justification by grace through faith alone.

Is your current belief system producing assurance, purpose, and peace, or is it bringing discouragement, disappointment, and despair? Jesus said that wisdom is shown to be right by what fruit results from it (cf. Matthew 11:19). Is your faith leading you in the right direction? Are you producing godly fruit? If not, consider who or what is leading you—religious tradition or a relationship with Jesus Christ?

As they say, "If you were arrested for being a Christian, is there enough evidence in your life to convict you?" Jesus said, "No one can serve two masters" (Matthew 6:24). Charles Spurgeon adds, "We cannot follow two things. If Christ be one of them, we cannot follow another." If He's not Lord, it may be because we have not yielded. Change occurs when there is a strong conviction of sin and genuine repentance. This shouldn't be discouraging but very encouraging ... God has provided the way. It's our choice to accept or reject it.

Who is Jesus? How we answer this question is the difference between right and wrong, light and darkness, heaven and hell. When asked this question, the Apostle

Peter gave the correct response: "You are the Christ, the Son of the living God" (Matthew 16:16). Jesus Himself confirmed this by saying: "I am the way, the truth, and the life. No one comes to the Father except through Me" (John 14:6).

Seriously consider who and what you choose to follow. We are sinners who need a Savior. Jesus came to seek and to save that which was lost. Hebrews 9:22 says that *without the shedding of blood, there is no removal of sin.* His blood was shed for our sins. We should be forever thankful.

We hear a great deal about God's judgment and what can keep us from heaven, and rightly so, because "the fear of the Lord is the beginning of knowledge" (Proverbs 1:7). But we also need to reflect on God's goodness, love, mercy, and grace. It's difficult to transmit my love for Jesus on these pages. He healed my brokenness and restored my life, and He can do the same for you. There is a deep longing inside all of us that cannot be satisfied until we recognize our need for a Savior and turn to Him. We must be *Desperate for More of Him.*

If current statistics hold true, many will continue to reject Christ, never to return, or they will embrace a glamorized Christianity, both to the same end. Life is a battleground not a playground! My goal, therefore, is not to be politically correct—it's to inspire you to change from the inside out. Many who are trapped in religion go through life lacking passion, direction, and purpose, often living with a sense of remorse and guilt. They wonder, "Have I been good enough?" A relationship with Christ changes that—2 Corinthians 5:17 states, "Therefore, if anyone is in Christ, he is a new creation; old things have passed away; behold, all things have become new." Your past is forgiven, your present secure, and your future certain. Through Christ, you are a brand new person. If you truly grasp hold of this truth, it can motivate and encourage you beyond measure. Though the road ahead may be uncertain at times, the solid ground beneath will never shift. It's all about Who you know.

You must be *Desperate for More of Him* ...

## EBook Sermon Links:

1. Are You Ready? [My Testimony]:
   https://vimeo.com/22000794

# APPENDIX 2: To Pastors—"Speak as a dying man to dying men."

A few years back, I listened in astonishment as some prominent "Christian leaders" talked about replacing "preaching" with "having a conversation." At first, I thought that they might be confusing individual conversations with how we should speak to the masses, but I was wrong. They felt that we should stop "preaching" from the pulpit and start being more passive and less confrontational. Never mind the fact that Jesus said, "I must preach the kingdom of God to the other cities also, because for this purpose I have been sent" (Luke 4:43). But according to many, it's time to replace the pulpit with a couch and preaching with conversing.

Don't get me wrong, I'm not questioning cosmetic issues such as styles of worship, ambiance, lighting, and mood. I'm challenging the dangerous practice of removing foundational principles—Spirit-empowered preaching is foundational. "Preaching is God's great institution for the planting and maturing of spiritual life. When properly executed, its benefits are untold; when wrongly executed, no evil can exceed its damaging results" (E.M. Bounds). Without the unction of the Holy Spirit, preaching has little effect, and we may find ourselves in the same place as Samson and the majority of the church today—*they know not that the Spirit of the Lord has departed from them* (cf. Judges 16:20).

There is a very troubling trend in the evangelical church as a whole. Foundational doctrines such as the cross, sin, judgment, and repentance were declared openly in the early hours of church history as well as in American history—when revivals and awakenings spread across our landscape.

Today, the truth is often neglected, watered-down, or avoided altogether in the hope of "not offending," "securing an audience," or being "user-friendly." Judgment is never mentioned; repentance is never sought; and sin is often excused. We want to build a church rather than break a heart; be politically correct rather than biblically correct; coddle and comfort rather than stir and convict. This leaves people confused and deceived because they believe in a cross-less Christianity that bears no resemblance to Jesus' sobering call to repentance. Even though not all are called to preach, we all are called to share God's Word with others—especially the difficult truths. Through this, we are then able to offer hope. Quoting Andrew Murray again, "To convince the world of the truth of Christianity, it must first be convinced of sin. It is only sin that renders Christ intelligible." In other words, Christianity only makes sense in light of the consequences of sin. **The good news about Christ can only be appreciated with the bad news as the backdrop.** *There are times when the saints must be fed, and there are times when the sinners must be warned* (C.H. Spurgeon). Preaching, witnessing, and teaching are to be done with God-given authority to truly be effective. When we fail to proclaim God's Word faithfully, we run the risk of "encouraging sin" and "perverting the words of the living God" (cf. Jeremiah 23).

Pastors are to be pillars who support truth, not who oppose it. Truth is not "flexible" when it comes to absolutes—it's solid and unyielding. Truth liberates. Truth rebuilds. Truth restores. Truth heals. Truth transforms. Truth prevails—we don't change truth—truth changes us!

Where are the Isaiahs and Jeremiahs calling nations to repentance? Where are the Peters and Pauls who spoke with such authority that martyrdom did not silence them? Though they are dead, they still speak! Where are the Wycliffs who stood so unyielding for the truth that he was called *The Morning Star of Reformation*? Where are the Tyndales and Huss' who were burned at the stake for simply declaring the truth? Where are the Luthers who, when asked to recant or face possible execution, said, "Here I stand; I can do no other"? Where are the John Calvins who shape the religious thoughts of our Western culture? Where are the John Knoxs who cried, "Give me Scotland [for the cause of Christ] or I die"? Where are the Whitefields who shook continents? Where are the Howell Harris', Daniel Rowlands', and Griffith Jones' who preached with such passion during the Welsh revivals of the 18th century that we still honor them today?

I say again, "Where are they?" Where are the John Wesleys who said, "Give me one hundred preachers who fear nothing but sin and desire nothing but God, and we will shake the gates of hell?" Where are the David Brainerds who spent so much time in prayer that even the great Jonathan Edwards was convicted? Where are the Robert Murray M'Cheynes who, even though he died at age twenty-nine, was one of Scotland's most anointed preachers—causing people to weep before even preaching a word (not emotionalism, but anointing)? Where are the Martin Luther King, Jr.s, who gave his life for a worthy cause? Where are the Spurgeons who spoke with such authority that his sermons are read more today than ever before? Where are the D.L. Moodys who brought America to her knees? Where are the Puritans like Richard Baxter who said, "I speak as a dying man to dying men"?

**Why is there a lack of conviction today? The reason may not only be in the pew, but in the pulpit as well.** Much depends on the prayer life of the preacher. Prayer is the first sign of a spiritually healthy church, and a spiritually healthy pastor. We don't need more marketing plans, demographic studies, or giving campaigns; we need men filled with the Spirit of God. Sermons shouldn't come from pop-psychology and the latest fad; they must come from the prayer closet where God prepares the messenger before we prepare the message. *It takes broken men to break men.*

Where are men with uncompromising power and authority in the pulpits today? Granted, there are some, and I appreciate their ministry, but as a whole, the church is lacking. The one thing that all of the great men previously mentioned had is the one thing that many are lacking—authority and the power of the Holy Ghost. They were also men of extraordinary prayer, brokenness, and humility. Men filled and clothed with power from on high. *The men who do the most for God are always men of prayer.* "Preaching, in one sense, merely discharges the firearm that God has loaded in the silent place" (Calvin Miller). **"Preaching is theology coming through a man who is on fire"** (D. Martyn Lloyd-Jones).

We'd do well to revisit Jeremiah 23 regularly. Although this passage was written primarily to the false leaders in Jeremiahs day, the principle still applies to us— stand firm in God's counsel:

> "'Woe to the shepherds who destroy and scatter the sheep of My pasture!' Says the LORD ... they also strengthen the hands of evildoers, so that no one turns back from his wickedness ... and to everyone who walks according to the dictates of his own heart, they say, 'No evil shall come upon you' .... I have not sent these prophets, yet they ran. I have not spoken to them, yet they prophesied ... but if they had stood in My counsel, and caused My people to hear My words, then they would have turned them from their evil way ... therefore, they shall not profit this people at all, says the LORD'" (Jeremiah 23:1-32).

These leaders, like many today, have "perverted the words of the living God" (vs. 36) by not warning, instructing, challenging, and contending for the faith. Pastor's, we must be *Desperate for More* ... Desperate for more of God ... Desperate for more of the Spirit's power ... Desperate for more brokenness and humility.

As the church falls deeper into self-reliance and further from reliance on God, our need for bold leadership has never been greater. Change will only occur when there is a strong conviction of sin, genuine faith, humility, and sincere repentance—may God grant us the wisdom and strength to proclaim these truths. We must stop confusing

God's patience with His approval and preach with conviction from the pulpits again.

Let it not be said of us today that there arose another generation after us who did not know the LORD because pastors failed to lead the people in the fear of the Lord. The burden of responsibility rests squarely upon our shoulders. **It's our choice—stand, or fall!**

## EBook Sermon Links:

1. A Message to the Pulpits of America
   [YouTube version]: http://www.youtube.com/
   watch?v=J2JJd7T9umA

# APPENDIX 3: Salvation—Sovereignty or Man's Responsibility?

There are primarily two differing beliefs concerning salvation—free will (man is free to accept or reject God's offer of salvation), or election (God elects only certain people for salvation).

A very popular practice among some free will advocates encourages unbelievers to say a quick prayer to avoid going to hell. Repentance is rarely sought, and belief in Jesus as Savior and Lord is minimized.

Is it the moving of our lips when we confess Jesus as Lord that secures redemption, or is it the condition of the heart? It's the heart. A quick gesture in the form of a prayer does not save if the heart has not repented and truly believed: "If you believe in your heart that God raised Him from the dead, you will be saved" (Romans 10:9). "Godly sorrow produces repentance leading to salvation" (2 Corinthians 7:10). Repentance and belief are essential!

A very popular practice on the other side is to avoid preaching the gospel as not to manipulate God's drawing of the elect. C.H. Spurgeon referred to this group as Hyper-Calvinists. He was criticized for statements such as, "The great error of Hyper-Calvinism is to neglect one side of the Word of God because it does not know how to explain both that God is effective and sovereign in all things and that man is free and responsible for all his actions."[38] Spurgeon said this during his famous sermon, *Sovereign Grace and Man's Responsibility*, delivered on

August 1st, 1858, "The system of truth is not one straight line, but two. No man will ever get a right view of the gospel until he knows how to look at the two lines at once." We won't know where these two lines of God's sovereignty and man's responsibility cross until eternity.

We are called to be faithful to the command to preach, witness, and proclaim the good news while understanding that God does the drawing, saving, and sealing. As I understand it, predestination/election is a process by which God, who lives outside of time, established certain parameters before the foundation of the world. He clearly called Noah to preach righteousness, Abraham to bring forth the Nation of Israel, and the Prophets to call nations to repentance (e.g., Jeremiah was called before he was even born). God called John the Baptist, filled with the Spirit from his mother's womb, to prepare the way of the Lord. God also predestined Jesus to die on the cross. Clearly, these events were predestined.

Ephesians 1:4-5 confirms both election and predestination: "Just as He chose us in Him before the foundation of the world, that we should be holy and without blame before Him in love, having predestined us to adoption as sons by Jesus Christ to Himself, according to the good pleasure of His will."

We cannot discard election and predestination anymore that we can discard our responsibility as seen in Romans 10:9, "If you confess with your mouth the Lord Jesus and believe in your heart that God has raised Him from the dead, you will be saved." We have a responsibility to confess, believe, and repent with the understanding that no one comes to Jesus unless the Father draws them (cf. John 6:44).

Romans 1:18-20 tells us that the wrath of God is being revealed against all who suppress the truth. Since the creation of the world God's invisible qualities—His eternal power and divine nature—have been clearly seen so that people are without excuse. Guilt often implies responsibility. "We are without excuse" because God's attributes are clearly seen; they bear witness to a Creator. Charles Hodge, in his classic work on systematic theology, spells it out plainly, "He [man] is a moral agent because he has the consciousness of moral obligation, and whenever he sins he acts freely against the convictions of conscience."[39]

In the act of salvation, God receives all the glory and all the credit. Salvation is His work, not ours. We are never outside of His sovereignty and control. But some ask, "Could God have created man to receive His offer of salvation or reject it?" Jesus said, in Mark 10:15, "Assuredly, I say to you, whoever does not receive the kingdom of God as a little child will by no means enter it." God is patient with us ... not wanting anyone to perish (cf. 2 Peter 3:9).

Without question, even the ability to receive is a gift from God, as is faith (cf. Ephesians 2:8). But does this mean that man does not have the ability to receive or reject the gift that is being offered? This ability, they say, does not make man good, quite the contrary, it makes him utterly dependant, desperate, and without hope unless he receives what God has offered (cf. Mk. 10:15).

1 Corinthians 2:14 states, "But the natural man does not receive the things of the Spirit of God, for they are

foolishness to him; nor can he know them, because they are spiritually discerned." The word "receive," or *dechomai* in the Greek, means to take hold of or to welcome. The natural man does not welcome the things of God, but did God give him the ability to accept or reject them? The answer to this question divides many. My heart is to see these two contending schools of theology be less divisive and more communicable. **Brother is shooting brother and friend is wounding friend.**

I like what Dr. Wayne Grudem said, "Exactly how God combines His providential control with our choices, Scripture does not explain to us. But rather than deny one aspect or the other (simply because we cannot explain how both can be true), we should accept both in an attempt to be faithful to the teaching of all of Scripture."[40] Contextually, Mr. Grudem is referring to choices that believers make, but the principle applies: how God combines providence with commands to repent and believe, is not crystal clear either. Yet, we are to accept both truths—man must repent and believe, but God's sovereign plans will prevail.

## EBook Sermon Links:

1. The New Civil War - Election or Free Will [YouTube version]: http://www.youtube.com/watch?v=Jqx_xfZ10rE

# ENDNOTES

1   John MacArthur, The Truth War, Nelson Books, 2007, pg. 2.

2   Ravi Zacharias, Jesus Among Other Gods, W Publishing Group, a Division of Thomas Nelson, Inc., 2000, p.50.

3   Wayne Grudem, Systematic Theology: An Introduction to Biblical Doctrine, Grand Rapids: Zondervan, 1994, p. 876.

4   John Calvin, Calvin's Commentaries—specifically Matthew 7.

5   John Gill, John Gill's exposition of the entire Bible—specifically Matthew 18.

6   John Wesley, John Wesley's Bible commentary—specifically 2 Thessalonians 3.

7   Oswald Chambers, The Complete Work of Oswald Chambers, Discovery House Publishers, 2000, p.3.

8   Wayne Grudem, Systematic Theology, Zondervan, 1994, pgs. 763-764.

9   Harry A. Ironside, in 1952, printed this illustration in his notes on the prophet Isaiah.

10  Edward Gibbon, The History of the Decline and Fall of the Roman Empire; published in six volumes.

11  Arturo G. Azurdia II gave a similar example in his book, Spirit Empowered Preaching. He deserves credit for this analogy.

12  J.C. Ryle, Holiness, Charles Nolan Publishers, 1877, p. 85.

13  J.C. Ryle, Holiness, Charles Nolan Publishers, 1877, p. 83-84.

14  E.M. Bounds, Power Through Prayer, Baker Book House, 1972, p. 9.

15 D.A. Carson, Becoming Conversant with the Emerging Church, Zondervan, 2005, p.44.

16 Oswald Chambers, The Complete Work of Oswald Chambers, Published by Discovery House Publishers, 2000, excerpt from Approved unto God, p.16.

17 Charles R. Swindoll, August 2004 edition, Insights newsletter, 2004. Published by Insight for Living, Plano, TX 75025, pgs.1-2.

18 This story appeared in ESPN The Magazine's Analytics issue on newsstands Feb. 22, 2013.

19 "It's Almost Too Late," New Man Magazine—interview with Josh McDowell, May/June, 2003, p. 56.

20 Craig Barnes, Sacred Thirst, Zondervan, 2000.

21 E.M. Bounds, Power Through Prayer, Baker Book House, 1972, p. 23.

22 Klyne Snodgrass, The NIV application commentary of Ephesians, Zondervan, Jun 26, 2009.

23 Excerpt from, The Temptation of Believers by Dr. John Owen.

24 C.H. Spurgeon, Ploughman Talks, Chapter Eight.

25 Duncan Campbell, The Price and Power of Revival (pamphlet), 1962, Chapter Three.

26 This excerpt is from an article entitled, True and False Fire, by George D. Watson. It was published at the beginning of the 1900s.

27 Charles Haddon Spurgeon, The Holy Spirit's Chief Office— sermon number 2382 delivered July 26th, 1888 at the Metropolitan Tabernacle, Newington.

28 D. Martyn Lloyd-Jones, from his sermon series on the Gifts and Baptism of the Holy Spirit.

29  Wayne Grudem, Systematic Theology, Zondervan, 1994, p. 1050.

30  J.C. Ryle, Holiness, Charles Nolan Publishers, 1877, p. 83-84.

31  Wayne Grudem, Systematic Theology, Zondervan, 1994, p. 1011.

32  The MacArthur Study Bible has an excellent outline illustrating genuine saving faith near the back of the Bible for those interested.

33  William C Martin, A Prophet With Honor—the Billy Graham Story, Quill, 1991, p.63.

34  Richard Owen Roberts, Repentance, Crossway, 2002, p. 21.

35  Matthew Henry's Concise Commentary on the Bible, 1 John 2.

36  Norman Grubb, Continuous Revival, CLC Publications, 1997, Chapter Two.

37  Mike Wilkerson, Redemption, Crossway, 2011, p. 31.

38  C.H. Spurgeon, Spurgeon v. Hyper-calvinism, Banner of Truth, 1995, p. 82.

39  Charles Hodge, Systematic Theology—volume II.

40  Wayne Grudem, Bible Doctrine: Essential Teachings of the Christian Faith, Zondervan, 1999, p. 146.